# Pharmaceutical Medicine and the Law

## Legal responsibility • Product liability • Europe

*Papers based on a conference organised by the
Faculty of Pharmaceutical Medicine of the Royal Colleges
of Physicians of the UK, April 1991*

Edited by
**Sir Abraham Goldberg**
*President, Faculty of Pharmaceutical Medicine;
Emeritus Regius Professor of the Practice of Medicine,
University of Glasgow*

**Ian Dodds-Smith**
*Partner, McKenna & Co, Solicitors, London*

1991

ROYAL COLLEGE OF PHYSICIANS OF LONDON
and
FACULTY OF PHARMACEUTICAL MEDICINE OF
THE ROYAL COLLEGES OF PHYSICIANS OF THE UK

**Acknowledgement**

The Royal College of Physicians is grateful to National Power Plc for their grant towards the publication of this book.

**Royal College of Physicians of London**
**11 St Andrew's Place, London NW1 4LE**

Typeset by Oxprint Ltd, Aristotle Lane, Oxford OX2 6TR
Printed by Cathedral Press Ltd, Salisbury, Wilts.

# Foreword

**Dame Rosalinde Hurley**
*Chairman, Medicines Commission*

---

Pharmaceutical Medicine and the Law is an important synthesis of the present law, both national and European, on the regulation and licensing of medicines and of related issues. The single European Act sets the date of 31 December 1992 for adoption by the European Community of programmes of legislation that complete the tasks set out in the Treaty of Rome. In view of the imminence of the date it is timely and apposite that many chapters in this book concentrate on European legislation and that others place European Community law and law-making in perspective for us within the context of United Kingdom law. The statement of Lord Denning (Chapter 10) that 'Community law . . . is part of our law which overrides any other part which is inconsistent with it . . .' is fundamental. The chapters that deal with Community law, with its complexities by way of Regulations or Directives, are not arid recitals of legislative detail but are lively and enlightening illustrations by the learned authors of the impact that the law-making Treaties of the Community have and will have on our mobilities and freedoms, particularly in respect of the free movement of medicines.

Of crucial importance to the subject or to the patient are the personal issues that may arise in ·the testing, prescription and acceptance of medicines. Here it is not always easy to separate legal from ethical requirements and both are addressed. The duties of pharmaceutical physicians are cardinal. The problem of consent both in research and in communication on medication is vexed and vexing, particularly where, in a telling phrase (Chapter 4), 'patients are already supplicants, if not mendicants'. Most medicines used are, of course, licensed but the special position of unlicensed medicines or of medicines used in unlicensed indications is discussed in a later chapter. Compensation and indemnity pose genuine problems: 'no fault compensation' has been highlighted recently by the unsuccessful Barnes Bill, and in an erudite debate in the House of Lords. The Report of the Royal College of Physicians of London on *Compensation for adverse consequences of medical intervention* is discussed, and its recommendations reprinted here. Multi-claimant actions for damages in negligence and the seeking of adjudication in the courts on allegations of wrongful acts by public bodies are increasing in the United Kingdom. These are important matters of public concern, of which few have direct experience; discussion on them can only be helpful.

Law and practice as it relates to pharmaceutical medicine and pharmaceutical products in the United Kingdom and Europe has been thoroughly reviewed and analysed in this book. We are all beholden to Sir Abraham Goldberg for inspiring it, and for the masterly essay that forms the first chapter.

# Editors' Preface

The Faculty of Pharmaceutical Medicine of the three Royal Colleges of Physicians of the United Kingdom was inaugurated on 26 October 1989. Members of the Faculty include doctors in the pharmaceutical industry, in the drug regulatory authority, as well as in academic medicine, particularly clinical pharmacology.

One of the functions of the Faculty is to promote discussion and learning of appropriate topics. To this end, it organised a one-day symposium, held on 23 April 1991, on *Pharmaceutical medicine and the law*. Health care, particularly medication, is so important to the community that the subject is hedged in by legal constraints. Awareness of the relevant laws is essential for all those actively involved in drug development, and it was for this group that the symposium was structured. The main topics emerged naturally: (1) the legal responsibilities of the pharmaceutical physician; (2) product liability and litigation; and (3) the European dimension.

The success of the conference encouraged the suggestion that a wider audience would be interested in the published proceedings. Three additional chapters were added: an historical perspective (chapter 1); the basis of liability of the licensing authority and its advisers under the Medicines Act (chapter 7); and, thirdly, unlicensed medicines and the use of drugs in unlicensed indications (chapter 8). Our aim is that this book may contribute to the understanding of a subject of growing interest and importance to doctors and lawyers.

We are grateful to Professor Sheila McLean, Professor Dame Rosalinde Hurley and Mrs Janice Webster for chairing the sessions; Professor Joseph M. Thomson for his summing up; the President, Visitor and Council of the Royal College of Physicians and Surgeons of Glasgow for providing generously the elegant precincts of the College in which the symposium was held; McKenna & Co., London, and Wright, Johnston & Mackenzie, Glasgow, for their support; and Mrs Ann Gascoine, Administrator of the Faculty of Pharmaceutical Medicine. Miss Diana Beaven of the Publications Department of the Royal College of Physicians, London, has been most helpful.

A.G. and I.D-S.

# Contributors

**Anthony Barton**
*Legal Assistant, McKenna & Co, Solicitors, London.*

**Noreen Burrows**
*Professor of European Law, University of Glasgow.*

**James P. Canlin**
*Barrister, Assistant Solicitor, Department of Health.*

**Euan F. Davidson**
*Managing Partner, Wright, Johnston & Mackenzie, Solicitors, Glasgow.*

**Ian Dodds-Smith**
*Partner, McKenna & Co, Solicitors, London.*

**Abraham Goldberg**
*President, Faculty of Pharmaceutical Medicine of the Royal Colleges of Physicians of the UK; Honorary Senior Research Fellow, Department of Modern History and Emeritus Regius Professor of the Practice of Medicine, University of Glasgow.*

**Leigh Hancher**
*Professor of Public Economic Law, Erasmus University, Rotterdam, The Netherlands.*

**Christopher Hodges**
*Partner, McKenna & Co, Solicitors, London.*

**Keith Jones**
*Chief Executive, Medicines Control Agency, London.*

**Ian Kennedy**
*Professor of Medical Law and Ethics, King's College, London.*

**Ronald D. Mann**
*Medical Services Secretary, Royal Society of Medicine, London Director, VAMP Research Ltd, London.*

**David Massam**
*Barrister, The Association of the British Pharmaceutical Industry, London.*

**Colin Milne**
*Partner, Wright, Johnston & Mackenzie, Solicitors, Glasgow.*

**Joseph M. Thomson**
*Regius Professor of Law, University of Glasgow.*

**Janice Webster**
*Director General, Council of Bars and Law Societies of the European Community.*

# Contents

|  |  | Page |
|---|---|---|
| **Foreword** *by Dame Rosalinde Hurley, Chairman, Medicines Commission* . . . . . . . . . | iii |
| **Editors' Preface** *by Sir Abraham Goldberg and Ian Dodds-Smith* | v |
| **Contributors** . . . . . . . . . | viii |

**1 Pharmaceutical medicine and the law: an historical perspective** *by Sir Abraham Goldberg* . . . . 1

| | |
|---|---|
| Introduction . . . . . . . . | 1 |
| Early medicine . . . . . . . . | 1 |
| India and China . . . . . . . | 1 |
| Mesopotamia and Egypt . . . . . | 2 |
| Greece and Rome . . . . . . | 2 |
| Arabia . . . . . . . . | 3 |
| The Middle Ages . . . . . . . | 3 |
| Mediaeval church . . . . . . | 3 |
| Salerno, London, Glasgow, Edinburgh . . . | 4 |
| Drugs from the New World . . . . . | 4 |
| The apothecaries . . . . . . . | 5 |
| Influence of chemistry . . . . . . | 5 |
| Scurvy: a controlled clinical trial . . . . | 6 |
| Smallpox vaccination . . . . . . | 6 |
| The lessons of digitalis . . . . . . | 7 |
| Chloroform . . . . . . . . | 7 |
| Drug legislation and therapeutic advances . . . | 8 |
| Origins of the drug explosion . . . . | 8 |
| Further drug legislation in the UK . . . . | 9 |
| Drug legislation in the USA . . . . | 9 |
| Thalidomide: legal consequences . . . . | 10 |
| Europe . . . . . . . . . | 11 |
| The European Free Trade Association (EFTA) . . | 11 |
| Conclusions . . . . . . . . | 12 |
| References . . . . . . . . | 13 |

**PART 1:**
**LEGAL RESPONSIBILITIES OF PHARMACEUTICAL**
**PHYSICIANS**

2  **Legal responsibilities of pharmaceutical physicians:**
   **view of ABPI** *by David Massam*   .        .        .        .        .        17
   Introduction.        .        .        .        .        .        .        .        17
   Promotion   .        .        .        .        .        .        .        .        18
   Certification of summaries   .        .        .        .        .        19
   Unlicensed medicines   .        .        .        .        .        .        21
   Fraud and misconduct in clinical trials   .        .        .        .        21
   Common sense   .        .        .        .        .        .        .        22
   References   .        .        .        .        .        .        .        .        22
   Discussion   .        .        .        .        .        .        .        .        22


3  **Legal responsibilities of pharmaceutical physicians:**
   **view of the Medicines Control Agency**
   *by James P. Canlin*   .        .        .        .        .        .        .        25
   Introduction.        .        .        .        .        .        .        .        25
   The Medicines Act 1968        .        .        .        .        .        25
   Product licence.        .        .        .        .        .        .        26
   Criminal law.        .        .        .        .        .        .        .        27
   Civil law        .        .        .        .        .        .        .        .        28
   Regulatory authorities   .        .        .        .        .        .        29
   Summary        .        .        .        .        .        .        .        .        30
   Discussion   .        .        .        .        .        .        .        .        30


4  **Consent and information: Research on healthy**
   **volunteers and patients** *by Ian Kennedy*   .        .        .        .        33
   Introduction.        .        .        .        .        .        .        .        33
   Ethics committees.        .        .        .        .        .        .        33
   Importance and validity of consent.        .        .        .        34
   Consent: general principles   .        .        .        .        .        34
   Law and guidelines        .        .        .        .        .        .        36
   The European Guidelines        .        .        .        .        .        36
   Informed consent .        .        .        .        .        .        .        37
   Requirements for consent        .        .        .        .        .        38
   Procedure for obtaining consent        .        .        .        .        39
   Research on the incompetent .        .        .        .        .        39
   Discussion .        .        .        .        .        .        .        .        40

**PART 2:**
**PRODUCT LIABILITY AND LITIGATION**
5   **Product liability issues arising out of the**
    **introduction of strict liability and procedures for**
    **dealing with multi-claimant cases** *by Ian Dodds-Smith* . 47
    Fault liability . . . . . . . . 47
    Strict liability . . . . . . . . 48
    Claims experience and changes in the legal environment . 48
    The practical effect of strict liability . . . 51
    Instructions for use and warnings . . . . 53
    Co-ordinated proceedings for multi-claimant cases . . 54
    Costs and cost-sharing . . . . . . 56
    Lead cases . . . . . . . . 57
    References and Notes . . . . . . 57
    Discussion . . . . . . . . 59

6   **Harmonisation of European controls over research:**
    **ethics committees, consent, compensation and**
    **indemnity** *by Christopher Hodges* . . . . 63
    Background . . . . . . . . 63
    Good Clinical Practice . . . . . . 65
    Comments on the European guidelines . . . 66
       Legal basis . . . . . . . 66
       GCP framework of ethics committees . . . 67
       Matters for consideration by an ethics committee . 69
    National development of ethics committees . . . 70
    Informed consent . . . . . . . 72
    Compensation . . . . . . . . 75
       Non-patient human volunteers: 1988 ABPI guidelines . 79
       Patient volunteers: 1991 ABPI guidelines . . 80
       Phase IV . . . . . . . . 83
       Volunteers . . . . . . . . 83
    Indemnities to investigators and institutions . . 84
    Insurance . . . . . . . . 84
    Legal responsibility of ethics committees . . . 85
    Conclusion . . . . . . . . 86
    References . . . . . . . . 86
    Discussion . . . . . . . . 88

7   **The basis of liability of the licensing authority and its**
    **advisers under the Medicines Act 1968 to an**
    **individual** *by Anthony Barton* . . . . 91
    Introduction . . . . . . . . 91
    The law . . . . . . . . 91

Public or private law? . . . . . . . 94
Tort . . . . . . . . . . 95
  Misfeasance . . . . . . . . 95
  Breach of statutory duty . . . . . 95
Negligence . . . . . . . . . 96
  Duty of care . . . . . . . . 96
  Breach of duty of care . . . . . . . 100
  Causation . . . . . . . . . 101
  Remoteness of damage in law . . . . . 101
Conclusions . . . . . . . . . 101

**8 Unlicensed medicines and the use of drugs in
unlicensed indications** *by Ronald D. Mann* . . . 103
The licensing provisions . . . . . . 103
  The Medicines Act 1968 . . . . . . 103
  Importing of unlicensed medicines . . . 105
  Personal clinical investigations . . . . 105
  The EEC Directives . . . . . . . 106
Types of unlicensed medicines . . . . . 106
Practical implications . . . . . . . 108
  Professional and product liability . . . . 108
  Data limitations . . . . . . . 109
  Labelling . . . . . . . . . 109
Summary . . . . . . . . . 110
References . . . . . . . . . 110

**9 Compensation for adverse consequences of medical
intervention: a legal view of the Royal College of
Physicians (London) report by** *by Colin Milne* . . 111
Introduction . . . . . . . . . 111
The Report . . . . . . . . . 112
  Introduction and Chapter 1 . . . . . 112
  Ch 2: Compensation under tort – causation, fault and
    quantum . . . . . . . . 113
  Ch 3: Evaluating the tort system . . . . 113
  Ch 4: Evaluating alternatives to tort . . . 114
  Ch 5: Options for reform . . . . . 114
  Ch 6: Conclusions and recommendations . . 115
  Summary . . . . . . . . . 117
Conclusion . . . . . . . . . 117
Appendix: Recommendations and summary of the Report
  (reprinted from the Report) . . . . . 118
Discussion . . . . . . . . . 120

**PART 3:**
**THE EUROPEAN DIMENSION**
    **Introduction to the European dimension:**
    *by Janice Webster* . . . . . . . 125


10   **The European Community: its structure and**
    **relationship with the UK** *by Euan F. Davidson* . . 127
    Introduction. . . . . . . . 127
    Sovereignty . . . . . . . . 127
    Supremacy of EC law . . . . . . 128
    The institutions of the EC . . . . . 130
        The Commission . . . . . . 130
        The Council of Ministers . . . . . 132
        The Parliament . . . . . . . 132
        The Courts . . . . . . . 133
    The legislative process . . . . . . 133
    The enforcement of EC law . . . . . 135


11   **The European Community interest in**
    **pharmaceuticals** *by Noreen Burrows* . . . 137
    Introduction. . . . . . . . 137
    Scenarios:
        1: the rejected practitioner . . . . . 137
        2: the rejected product . . . . . 138
        3: the frustrated whizz-kids. . . . . 138
        4: the protective state . . . . . . 138
    The legal rules . . . . . . . 138
    The free movement of persons . . . . 139
    The free movement of goods . . . . . 139
    Competition law . . . . . . . 140
    Public procurement . . . . . . 141
    Conclusions . . . . . . . . 141
    References . . . . . . . . 142


12   **Parallel imports and EC law** *by Leigh Hancher* . . 143
    Introduction. . . . . . . . 143
    Pricing and reimbursement . . . . . 144
    Harmonisation of safety legislation. . . . 146
    Patent protection: the new proposals . . . 151
    Conclusion . . . . . . . . 153
    Notes . . . . . . . . . 154

**13  European drug regulatory integration** *by Keith Jones*   .      157
      Introduction.      .      .      .      .      .      .      .      157
      The European pharmaceutical Directives      .      .      .      158
            Directive 75/318/EEC      .      .      .      .      .      .      158
            Directive 75/319/EEC      .      .      .      .      .      .      158
            Directive 87/22/EEC .      .      .      .      .      .      159
            Extension Directives .      .      .      .      .      .      159
      Current and future legislation      .      .      .      .      .      159
      Future licensing arrangements      .      .      .      .      .      161
      Conclusion   .      .      .      .      .      .      .      .      163

**14  Summary** *by Joseph M. Thomson*      .      .      .      .      .      165

# 1 | Pharmaceutical medicine and the law: an historical perspective

**Sir Abraham Goldberg**

*President, Faculty of Pharmaceutical Medicine of the Royal Colleges of Physicians of the UK, and Honorary Senior Research Fellow, Department of Modern History, University of Glasgow*

## Introduction

Pharmaceutical medicine may be defined as the development, evaluation and monitoring of medicines and their marketing. Although it matured as a medical specialty just over 20 years ago, its origins and its association with the law can be traced from earliest times. Disease was considered by primitive man to be of supernatural origin, a thunderbolt from the gods. Treatment, bringing freedom from disease, was the monopoly of the gods who therefore had to be placated before relief could be obtained. Increasingly, man took over this god-like role, often using herbs and natural products, and the community grudgingly accepted his skills but imposed legal constraints on his divinely abrogated powers.

In primitive societies today, for example, the American Indians and the Africans of the Congo, it is evident that a 'doctor' does not have to be uniformly successful in his treatments, but is vulnerable in the event of failure only if his medical procedures do not conform to the standards of the community.[1] Much of early medicine reflected the development of agriculture and culture along the great rivers—the Indus, Tigris, Euphrates and the Nile—as well as in China and, later, Greece.

## Early medicine

### India and China

Ayudervic medicine in India contained a voluminous pharmacopoeia, a few examples of which, eg rauwolfia serpentina, have been adopted for modern use. The Laws of Manu were rules for early life and ritual, compiled about 200 BC—AD 200; they stated that the physician could be penalised for improper treatment.[1] The Chinese Emperor Shen

Nung, about 5,000 years ago, recorded some 365 drugs in the Great Herbal, many of which he tested on himself. Most of them are now obsolete but some, such as opium and arsenic, have survived. Another, Ma Huang, was the drug from which ephedrine was isolated in the 20th century. Cannabis indica was used by the Chinese as a narcotic draught for anaesthesia. The same principle of discipline for physicians can be seen in the Chinese Institutions of Chou, written several centuries before Christ. Each physician had to report his results, success or failure, which determined his progress up and down the five grades of the hierarchical ladder of physicians. Academics were not exempt from this form of audit, and a fine would be imposed upon a professor if his student attendance was poor or if the students did badly in examinations.

## *Mesopotamia and Egypt*

The code of King Hammurabi of Mesopotamia, written on a large piece of stone several thousand years old, can be seen in the Louvre in Paris, and provides evidence of an ancient regulatory system. Engraved on this stone are several hundred codicils or laws relating to medicine and surgery. For instance, if a slave's eye was destroyed by a surgeon, the surgeon had to pay half the price of the slave in silver; if he damaged a nobleman's eye, the surgeon could lose his hands. Egyptian medicine and therapeutics dominated the ancient world for 2,000 years. The Ebers Papyrus, compiled about 1550 BC and discovered in 1862, contained 811 different medicinal formulas concocted by priest physicians, including castor oil, myrrh and frankincense. Rigid controls of the system were laid down in the Sacred Book. If the patient died and the practitioner had deviated in any major fashion from the basic tenets, he was submitted to a trial with death as a possible penalty.

## *Greece and Rome*

Greek medicine has two main components: the more ancient Temple Medicine (or what we would now call alternative medicine) and Hippocratic (or rational scientific medicine). In the *Odyssey* Homer remarked on the healing nature of some drugs and on others which could be harmful. Drugs are seldom mentioned in the Hippocratic writings. We can read 'In acute disease employ drugs very seldom; never prescribe them until you have made a thorough examination of the patient'. Occasionally a drug is mentioned, for example hellebore, 'a dangerous drug which might induce convulsions'. We know that the Greeks appreciated the importance of monitoring drugs from a commemorative stone on the Acropolis in Athens which records that in the 4th century BC Evanor, the physician, was chosen as Inspector of Drugs. The sophisticated Roman civilisation was correctly cynical of medicines, of treatment and of doctors. The Romans developed techniques for detecting adulteration of drugs, as recorded in the materia medica of Dioscorides. Among his methods for analysis were drug solubility, specific gravity and reaction to ignition. Galen's use of plant medication was adhered to for nearly 1,500 years and was incorporated into Arabic medicine. Interestingly, he warned against badly written and obscure prescriptions.

## *Arabia*

In mediaeval Moslem countries, the office of the Hisba in the early 9th century enforced religious codes of public morality, but in addition sent out officials with specific instructions to inspect the syrups and drugs of the apothecaries' shops at any time of the day or night. These inspectors, trained as apothecaries, reported on infringements of the rules which could lead to punishment, including heavy fines, the pillory and the bastinado (the lashing of the soles of the feet with wooden canes).

## The Middle Ages

### *Mediaeval Church*

Throughout the mediaeval period the church made great efforts to alleviate the suffering of the sick by the institution of hospices and hospitals, and by encouraging the compassion if not the science of medicine. Many monasteries had their own herbal gardens and physicians were schooled in the seminaries of the Holy Church. With the rise of non-monastic schools of medical learning, monks were prohibited from participating in such centres. The most important of such prohibitions was the decree of the Council of Tours in 1163, which was subsequently included in various canon law collections. This prohibition was greatly expanded by a papal decree of 1219 forbidding secular clergy in responsible positions from absenting themselves from their ecclesiastical duties in order to study medicine or law. The 4th Lateran Council in 1215 forbade the use of any medical treatment by 'sinful' means, for example, giving prescription to eat meat on fast days or advice to engage in sexual intercourse outside marriage.

## Salerno, London, Glasgow, Edinburgh

The school of Salerno was the prototype of the modern European medical schools and flowered over the period of the crusades (1096–1270). It was in Salerno that the control of the quality of medicines and their standards first began in Europe in the modern era. These concepts moved to the Low Countries, Germany and France, and later to England and Scotland in the 15th and 16th centuries. In 1224, the Hohenstaufen Emperor, Frederick II, ordered the regular inspection of apothecaries' drugs, warning them that they could forfeit their own life if a consumer died.[2] As early as 1423 the city authorities of London appointed drug inspectors. In 1540, Henry VIII empowered the Royal College of Physicians (which he had founded 22 years previously) to appoint four Fellows as inspectors of apothecaries' wares in the London area and to ensure that drugs were both pure in preparation and being administered efficaciously.

Four years prior to becoming James I of the combined realm in 1603, James VI of Scotland started a Faculty of Physicians and Surgeons in Glasgow. One of the important functions of the Faculty was the regulation of medicines, since many people had died as a result of adulterated drugs. The Edinburgh Pharmacopoeia was published in the late 17th century, and its early editions were used by physicians to exert their authority to control drugs and to attempt to limit the growing power of the apothecaries.

## Drugs from the New World

Just as in an earlier period Indian and Chinese medicine and knowledge of pharmaceuticals were dispersed over Asia and later through the Arabs to Europe, so the expeditions to the New World some 500 years ago provided the vehicle for the importation of new pharmaceuticals. Nicolas Monardes, in the 16th century, an Italian who lived in Spain, obtained specimens of many plants imported from 'New Spain' and Central America. He was the first to write about curare and guaiacum and tobacco (the last long before Sir Walter Raleigh). He gave the earliest account of the effects of the leaves of the coca bush, the divine plant of the Incas, used by them to allay fatigue, and from which cocaine was isolated in 1860. This was to prove a mixed blessing for our generation, with its many legal implications. In the 17th century, Count Cinchona, Spanish viceroy to Lima, Peru, brought back to Spain 'fever bark', from which quinine was eventually isolated. Tobacco was originally used in the New World as a preventive and treatment of syphilis. In a number of respects it can be classified as a drug; nicotine, of course, has specific pharmacological properties. James, King of England and Scotland, hated tobacco and lambasted its evil effects in his famous pamphlet, *Counterblaste to Tobacco*. Less well known is that in 1616 he legislated against smoking in Scotland, unsuccessfully, because 'the use or abuse of taking tobacco is lately croppin within Scotland, ane weede so infective as all young and ydill personis are in a mainer bewitchet thairwith'. This law had no effect on the smoking habits of the Scots. James' interest in medicine may have been stimulated by his teacher George Buchanan who had written a colourful history of Scotland in which he stated that Josina, supposedly the 9th King of Scotland, obtained his education in Ireland and wrote a thesis on 'the virtue and power of herbs'.

## The apothecaries

Until the early 17th century the apothecaries of London were members of the Grocers Company. As they grew in knowledge, skill and importance, they visited patients and gave treatment that doctors prescribed. They resented being controlled by the grocers, and sought separation from them through Gideon Delaune, a Frenchman who had compounded a famous pill and was apothecary to Queen Anne (James I's wife). Separation from the grocers was initially attempted through an Act of Parliament, and finally achieved in 1617 after a petition to the King who was influenced by his personal physician, the Huguenot Sir Theodor de Mayerne.

## Influence of chemistry

The dominant treatments from ancient times were herbals and natural products. In the 16th century Paracelsus burned the books of Galen in his rebellion against the inefficacy of plant medication: 'the body is made of chemicals; use chemicals to treat disease'. He could be called the pioneer of chemotherapy, and was certainly the founder of pharmaceutical chemistry. He pointed to the importance of extraction of the 'arcanum' or active principle, from the crude drug. The 17th and 18th centuries saw the growth of chemistry, clinical medicine and the relevance of scientific biology: Robert Boyle, the great chemist and founder of analytical chemistry; Von Haller, the Swiss physician and physiologist; Joseph Black, the Scottish physician and chemist, discoverer of carbon dioxide; and Scheele, the Swedish chemist. The paradox between the advancement of science and drug therapy is illustrated by the example of Robert Boyle, who provided the foundations of his subject in *The Sceptical Chemist*, published in 1661. He also wrote *A Collection of Choice Remedies* in 1691, describing a hotchpotch of messes with ingredients such as worms, horse dung, human urine, and moss from a dead man's skull. Although the therapeutic rewards were small at that time, these scientific advances were an essential basis for the drug discoveries of the 19th and 20th centuries.

## Scurvy — a controlled clinical trial

The scientific influence of the mid-18th century was the necessary background to James Lind's controlled experiment on scurvy, then a common disease in the British Navy. Lind, an Edinburgh graduate, was a surgeon's mate in 1747 when he carried out on 12 scorbutic sailors on HMS Salisbury in the English Channel what was probably the first controlled clinical trial. There were six pairs of patients, and each pair was given a different treatment. Lind found 'sudden and visible effects from the use of oranges and lemons', in the two patients given these.[3] They got better in one week. Impressed by Lind's studies, Captain James Cook added citrus juice to the diet of the sailors of his South Sea voyage of 1772–75, and reported its unprecedented success to the Royal Society in 1776. Despite these remarkable and convincing studies made by officers in the Royal Navy, the use of citrus juice (as lime juice) was not officially adopted by the Navy until 1795, over 40 years after the publication of Lind's treatise in 1753. Transposed to the late 20th century, one could imagine the dramatic legal scenario of multi-claimant litigation raised by the hundreds of widows of sailors who had died needlessly from scurvy as a result of negligence of the Lords of the Admiralty, blind to the 'state of the art'.

## Smallpox vaccination

One year after the tardy introduction of lime juice by the Navy, the greatest advance in the treatment of infection took place, only to be equalled in importance 150 years later by the introduction of penicillin. Edward Jenner transferred the cowpox virus from a lesion in the hand of a milkmaid, Sarah Nelmes, and inoculated some of it into the skin of eight year old James Phipps in May 1796. Later he inoculated the boy with virulent smallpox pus to which, most happily, James did not react. In considering his report on this work involving 23 case histories, one is amazed, affected by our 20th century regulations, at the massive confidence of Jenner, to do it without a clinical trial certificate or exemption or parental written consent. Would he have obtained permission today for such a study—without knowledge of the quality of the inoculated substance and in the absence of animal studies?

## The lessons of digitalis

Perhaps the teaching of the pharmacological significance of botany by Von Haller, Boerhaeve of Leyden, and Cullen of Scotland provided the most immediate reward in the epochal discovery of digitalis by William Withering in 1775. Withering, the son of an apothecary, was well taught in Edinburgh by Cullen on the importance of botany to medicine. When he eventually settled in Edgbaston near Birmingham his observations on the foxglove came to a mind well prepared. He wrote:

> In the year 1775 a Shropshire old woman was known to have a treatment for dropsy (oedema). This medicine was composed of 20 or more herbs, but it was not very difficult for me to perceive that the active herb could be none other than foxglove—digitalis purpurea.

Based on his observations over the next 10 years, he wrote in 1785 *An account of the foxglove and some of its medical uses*. In this work he identified the proper indications for digitalis, differentiating cardiac from other causes of oedema. He also ascertained the correct dosage range and adverse reactions of the drug. Withering was aware that because of its narrow therapeutic range, digitalis often did harm as well as good. Indeed deaths occurred from overdosage and Withering himself feared 'that a medicine of so much efficacy should be condemned and rejected as dangerous and unmanageable'.[4] Withering's work survived this difficulty, and the drug is still in use today. Thus, a pattern emerges of scientific advances, bringing improvements in treatment but also adverse effects and the dangers associated with them. This pattern, so clearly shown with digitalis over 200 years ago, is of vital importance to pharmaceutical medicine and the law at the present day.

## Chloroform

Another example of this pattern is chloroform, introduced by James Simpson of Edinburgh in 1847. Its use became commonplace after it was applied during the birth of Queen Victoria's seventh child. In terms of painless childbirth, chloroform was a great advance but it was not long before a series of deaths occurred due to complications, in all probability ventricular fibrillation of the heart. The number of fatalities was such that in 1877 the British Medical Association (BMA) set up a commission to investigate the problem.[5]

## Drug legislation and therapeutic advances

Two years before the BMA's action Benjamin Disraeli's government had broken new ground in the regulation of food and drugs with the introdution of the Sale of Food and Drugs Act of 1875. No statute had been enacted on a related topic since the Gin Acts of the 18th century. The 1875 Act became the competent legal basis for regulation until 1928, when there was clearly a need for further regulation because of the burgeoning growth of new drugs emanating from Europe, particularly Germany.

### *Origins of the drug explosion*

The development of new drugs had its origins at the beginning of the 19th century with the isolation of active principles from plant medication, such as morphine (1804), strychnine (1818) and quinine (1820). In addition, scientific pharmacology was pioneered by Bucheim, in Tartu, Estonia (1846), and his pupil, Schmiedeberg, in Strasbourg (1872), a city which had been transferred to the Germans after the Franco-Prussian war, and where they proudly built up an international pharmacology school.

Until 1880 medicines were obtained only from natural products, but Von Stradonitz in Germany then developed the benzene ring theory. This led to dye production from coal tar and became the basis of the chemical and pharmaceutical industries with the organic synthesis of new drugs. This was the real beginning of the drug explosion of the 20th century, and was made possible by brilliant collaboration between university and industry and considerable German investment in research and development.

At about the same time in France, the Germ Theory of Louis Pasteur, once accepted, had profound effects on the medical, scientific and lay communities. The fact that he was a chemist, not a doctor, emphasised the importance of science in the conquest of disease. He was to provide a seminal influence to the work of Koch, Metchnikoff and Ehrlich. The most important development was Paul Ehrlich's discovery of arsphenamine (606) for the treatment of syphilis, then the scourge of the modern world, in 1909, in Frankfurt. Sadly, that treatment had several serious adverse effects—liver failure, allergic responses and death. What had been a triumph turned into a nightmare. In typical fashion Ehrlich set to work, and eventually introduced neo-arsphenamine (914) which, though less effective, was less toxic than 606.[6]

## Further drug legislation in the UK

Ehrlich also made pioneering discoveries in blood diseases, immunology and cancer research. His contributions, those of Karl Landsteiner in 1901, which made blood transfusion possible by the discovery of blood groups, and of Banting and Best with the discovery of insulin in 1921, were the essential preludes to the Therapeutic Substances Act of 1925. This Act controlled medicinal products of biological origin, such as vaccines, sera, blood products and insulin.

Other statutes were passed to deal with the problems of drugs and disease: the Venereal Disease Act, 1917, the Cancer Act, 1939, and the Dangerous Drugs Act, 1930. The last Act was amended until 1965, and was eventually superseded in 1971 by the Misuse of Drugs Act. Each Act recognised certain dangers to the community, for example, drug addiction and irresponsible advertising of drugs for serious disorders.

## Drug legislation in the USA

The thread of our story must return to 1936, the year of Domagk's discovery of red prontosil, the herald of the sulphonamide group of drugs, shortly to be followed by the discovery of penicillin for therapeutic use in 1940. This started a chain reaction for the discovery of antibiotics which proceeds to this day. Again, the sequence is clear, with discovery of new drugs, therapeutic advance, recognition of adverse reactions and legal consequences. In the USA in 1937, the introduction of an elixir of sulphanilamide containing the toxic and lethal solvent diethylene glycol caused the death of more than 100 patients. This led to important changes in US medical and pharmaceutical law. From about 1880 onwards the US Department of Agriculture had submitted more than 100 Bills to Congress for the purpose of regulating food and drugs, none of which was approved until the Food and Drugs Act in 1906. This empowered the Department of Agriculture to regulate adulterated products (medicines or foods containing harmful materials) and misbranded products (medicines or foods claiming to contain active ingredients which they did not). Safety or efficacy testing by the manufacturer was not required.

After the tragic experience of the elixir of sulphanilamide, the original Act was repealed and replaced by the Food, Drug and Cosmetic Act in 1938. This established requirements for the registration and safety testing of new drugs by the manufacturer and for factory inspections. In 1951, an amendment to the Act established the requirement for the regulation of prescription drugs. It may be that this tightening of the regulation that followed the elixir of sulphanilamide tragedy protected the USA from the thalidomide disaster. In 1962, the Kefauver-Harris amendment, approved by Congress, introduced requirements for pre-marketing submission of both safety and efficacy data to the Food and Drug Administration (FDA). These requirements included investigational new drug applications (IND) and new drug applications (NDA) (which correspond to the UK clinical trial certificate and product licence applications, respectively).

## Thalidomide: legal consequences

The most harrowing association of pharmaceutical medicine and the law was the experience of thalidomide, which led to a global appreciation of the necessity for drug regulation on a much firmer basis than had ever previously been considered. Although there had been some preliminary observations of the neurotoxicity of thalidomide, an effective hypnotic not disallowed in pregnancy, in 1961–62 Lenz found a gross excess of congenital malformations and that thalidomide taken by the mother in pregnancy was the common factor in these cases. He communicated this message to a group of paediatricians in Hamburg, some of whom were able to endorse his observations. Chemie Grunenthal was the small German company that manufactured thalidomide. A legal issue has been whether the state of the art of drug testing should have been able to predict such an appalling adverse effect. Certainly the technical facilities for such testing existed, but it is most unlikely that the standard or routine tests used by the main manufacturers at that time would have detected the teratogenic potential.[7]

A consequence in the UK was the establishment of the Committee on Safety of Drugs (CSD) in 1963, with Sir Derrick Dunlop as chairman. The CSD dealt entirely with safety and some aspects of quality, but not with efficacy. Dunlop stated in 1967, 'the Committee's remit does not impose upon it any responsibility to consider the efficacy of drugs, except insofar as their safety is concerned'. In Norway and Sweden, however, there was relevant legislation dating from 1928 and 1935, respectively, which gained experience with systems to assess the efficacy of new drugs, while the Kefauver-Harris amendment to the US Drug Law of 1962 required the pre-market submission of both efficacy and safety data to the FDA.

In the UK, the Medicines Act of 1968 included efficacy as well as safety and quality as a tripartite basis for the benefit-risk judgement of new drugs. It also laid down that the appropriate committee—the Committee on Safety of Medicines (CSM)—should promote 'the collection and investigation of information relating to adverse reactions for the purpose of enabling it to give advice on the safety, quality and efficacy of medicinal products'. The yellow card system of adverse drug reaction monitoring by voluntary reporting of doctors and dentists has progressively gained strength since its inception in 1964 and there are now over 20,000 reports annually.

Despite all the experience gained by the CSD and CSM since 1963, the introduction of a number of new drugs has been associated with major problems. For example, the oculo-muco-cutaneous syndrome of practolol took a wearisome four years to unfold, the only one of the most valuable group of beta-blockers to cause this problem. Even in retrospect this problem was unpredictable, as was the vaginal cancer in daughters whose mothers had taken diethylstilboestrol during their pregnancy 15–20 years previously or the tragedy of acquired immune deficiency syndrome (AIDS) caused by contaminated blood and blood products administered in the 'unaware period' of the early 1980s.

## Europe

In Europe the post-war period saw an expanding drug industry, with a general increase in drug safety regulations. With the formation of the European Economic Community (EEC) in 1957 under the Treaty of Rome, there was no specific regulation for drugs in the Treaty. In 1965, however, the first of the Community pharmaceutical Directives was adopted, and subsequent amendments and additions now provide a detailed framework (to be completed by 1992) for the marketing of medicines in Member States. In 1975, the EEC introduced a specific medicinal advisory body for human medicines, the Committee for Proprietary Medicinal Products (CPMP). This provides a forum for considering marketing authorisation on a Community-wide basis, but its opinions are not binding and it has not been found to be an ideal instrument for mutual recognition of products. In 1987, the Community adopted a new Directive whereby the CPMP will consider applications for new products of biotechnology, the so-called High Technology Directive, prior to their evaluation and grant of a marketing authorisation by the Member States. This would seem to be a first step towards a centralised European regulatory authority—a draft Regulation published in 1990 is now under active discussion. Some form of supranational drug regulatory system is bound to be established (a subject which is fully discussed in Chapter 13 by Dr Keith Jones).

### The European Free Trade Association (EFTA)

This association includes Austria, Finland, Norway, Sweden and Switzerland. Since 1965 moves towards the recognition of scientific data have taken place, and in 1979 a scheme was introduced for the mutual recognition of evaluation reports of pharmaceutical products. The East European countries have the Council of Mutual Economic Assistance (CMEA) which, prior to the recent disintegration of the Warsaw Pact, provided co-operation on pharmaceutical developments. The present status of the CMEA is not known.

## Conclusions

An historical perspective has been applied to the developments of 'pharmaceutical medicine' and the laws which relate to treatment, mainly drug treatment of disease. Advances in drug therapy bring benefits but always some risk of adverse effect, for the only totally safe drug is an inert one. The law in its various forms has always followed the drug advance, reacting to the adverse changes created by the innovation. Several factors promote advances in drug discovery and development: *a sophisticated society*, as in the Rome of the Emperor Marcus Aurelius, when his physician Galen laid the basis of plant medication which was to last 1,500 years; *the exploration of new continents*, as in the importation to Europe of drugs from the New World in the 16th century; *a period of scientific enlightenment*, as in that of the 17th and 18th centuries, yielding the rich harvest of Withering's digitalis and the drugs of the 19th and 20th centuries. In addition, the *Great Wars* forced the pace of drug and therapeutic development, for example, the pressure on the development and manufacture of the arsenicals for the treatment of syphilis in the first world war, and of penicillin and synthetic antimalarials in the second; great *technological advances*, for example, molecular biology, particularly applied to genetic engineering of new proteins. Legal and ethical consequences follow these advances, just as the behaviour pattern of the permissive society of the 1960s was facilitated by the oral contraceptive pill.

To cope with the increase in pharmaceutical and medical litigation, a distinguished group of specialists in pharmaceutical and medical law and ethics has emerged both in the universities and legal practice. But this expansion of a medical-legal specialty had an early pioneer over 200 years ago in François Chaussier (1746–1828),[8] one of the remarkable Frenchmen brought to prominence by the French Revolution. He initiated the study of law in relation to medicine and assembled legal cases involving accidents, damage claims, liability and negligence in a comprehensive study for the first time. When medical training in France was restored in 1794, Chaussier influenced the introduction of legal medicine into the curriculum.

Has the method of historical perspective any contribution to make to the solution of problems of pharmaceutical law? The brilliant pageant of medical discovery over the last 100 years has been punctuated by some misfortunes: 'the longer you can look back, the further you can look forward',[9] and the less likely are you to repeat the mistakes of the past. Finally, an appreciation of the development of drug innovation and the limitations of the state of scientific and technological knowledge at the relevant period in time is an essential prerequisite for the just resolution of a legal controversy in pharmaceutical medicine.

## References

1. Lyons, AS and Pettrocelli, RJ (1978) *Medicine — an illustrated history.* Harry N Abrams Inc, New York.
2. Davies, DM (1985) *Textbook of adverse drug reactions.* 3rd Edn. Oxford University Press, Oxford.
3. Lind, James (1753) *A treatise of the scurvy.* Edinburgh.
4. Mann, RD (1985) *William Withering and the foxglove.* MTP Press Ltd, Lancaster.
5. McKendrick, JG, Coats, J and Newman, D (1880) Report of the action of anaesthetics. *Brit. Med. J.* **ii**, 957.
6. Medical Research Council (1922) *Toxic effects following the employment of arsenobenzol preparations.* Special Report. Series No. 66.
7. Sneader, W (1985) *Drug discovery: the evolution of modern medicines,* p32. John Wiley and Sons, Chichester, New York.
8. Vess, DM (1975) *Medical revolution in France 1789–1796.* University Presses of Florida. Gainesville.
9. Moran, Lord and Churchill, WS (1944) *Lancet,* 11 March.

## Part 1

---

# Legal responsibilities of
# pharmaceutical physicians

# 2 | Legal responsibilities of pharmaceutical physicians: view of ABPI

**David Massam**

*Barrister, The Association of the British Pharmaceutical Industry, London*

## Introduction

What is the view of The Association of the British Pharmaceutical Industry (ABPI) as regards pharmaceutical physicians and the law? Doubtless it is that they ought to comply with it. The converse is rather more noteworthy: because a particular action is not illegal does not mean one ought to do it (I stress that these are my personal observations).

The pharmaceutical physician and the law may be looked at in three ways:

1. Possible criminal liability on the part of the doctor personally and/or the employing company.
2. Possible civil liability on the part of the doctor personally and/or the company.
3. The responsibility or duty, ethical or legal, of the doctor to detect or prevent breaches of the criminal or civil law by others.

It is not always easy to separate legal and ethical requirements. For example, in relation to promotion, the Association's Code of Practice for the Pharmaceutical Industry[1] is much more comprehensive than the corresponding advertising regulations[2] of the Medicines Act 1968 itself. Some matters will be breaches both of the law and of the Code and some only of one or the other.

There are, or course, many circumstances in which a company may break the law, from running vehicles with tyres with inadequate treads to the many possibilities under the Medicines Act, some of which carry severe penalties including prison. Individual employees of the company may be personally in breach of the criminal law for activities carried out during the course of their employment. As is well known, a doctor employed in the pharmaceutical industry was found guilty of a criminal offence a few years ago in relation to misleading promotional information. This incident certainly served to concentrate the minds of doctors in the industry and to make them much more concerned than previously about possible personal liability. (I shall refer to promotion in some detail later.) There are other possibilities; for example, the Copyright, Designs and Patents Act 1988, which considerably tightened up the penalties for breach of copyright, can now lead to a fine or imprisonment for such a breach, and this would be a personal offence on the part of whoever committed it. Both the company and the individual employee can be responsible in relation to civil matters. A plaintiff who felt that a specific employee was particularly responsible for an event complained of might join the employee and the company together in his action.

I propose to deal specifically with a few particular issues.

## Promotion

Many pharmaceutical physicians will be called upon to certify advertisements in relation to the pharmaceutical industry's Code of Practice. This means that, having examined the material, they believe it is in accordance with the requirements of the advertising regulations, consistent with the product licence and the data sheet, and a fair and truthful representation of the facts about the product. There was a lot of argument about the wording when this was first put into the Code in 1978. It does not mean that the material must be correct, but that the signatory reasonably believes it to be in order: that he or she has examined it in a rational manner and, with the benefit of appropriate background knowledge and experience, is able to come to an informed opinion on the matter and decide whether or not to certify. In the case of straightforward misjudgement without negligence or malice, it seems unlikely that any personal liability would ensue as far as either the criminal law or the Code of Practice was concerned.

The signatory needs to be able to step back from an advertisement to some extent and look at it as others will see it. This will help him or her not to fall into the trap resulting from being too familiar with the material, which may lead to possibly significant information being omitted that seems obvious to those who prepare and approve the promotional material but which may not be so obvious to those who read it. It should not be assumed that the readers are as familiar with the subject as the signatory.

It should be remembered that the Code of Practice can be breached even when the statement in question turns out to be true. This arises at the forefront of clinical experience when it may reasonably be thought that a particular thing is true but it is not yet sufficiently firmed up to be regarded as established. The situation can therefore arise where a statement may well be true but there is no proper substantiation for it and it is therefore in breach of the Code. Another point to remember is that the signatory can be called upon to provide evidence to substantiate any statement in promotional material, and that the person requesting it may well be the medical director of a competitor company — in fact he or she probably will be. It is a useful mental exercise when writing or certifying promotional material to consider what would be supplied in relation to each particular claim were substantiation to be sought. Is the evidence good enough? If there is nothing available which would substantiate a claim, it cannot be made.

A further problem that can arise is the gradual expanding claim. In some areas of medicine, where particular conditions are part of a wider spectrum of similar or related conditions, it may be that a product is initially established only for one facet of it and later proves to be of use in others. There have been instances when extra shades of use have been claimed inch by inch until suddenly the company has taken a mile and is accused of promoting indications which are not covered by the product licence at all. Everything for which the product is recommended must be consistent with the product licence.

It has to be accepted that those certifying advertisements may be subjected to pressures within the company. It is a hard world, but in the end the certifying physician may have to stand up for what he or she believes to be right. Is the medical director the company conscience or the company lackey? Hopefully, he or she is someone who can take a balanced view of things, someone who can see the need to promote medicines in a positive way but who, on the other hand, is mindful of the special nature of medicines and able to take a responsible line to ensure that patients are never put at risk. Patients must be the main concern of the Code of Practice Committee. Other companies are of course aggrieved when they see themselves disadvantaged by their competitors' advertising. The prime concern, however, must be to safeguard the interests of patients. In my experience, few, if any, of the breaches of the Code which I have seen over the years would have had any effect on patient safety.

## Certification of summaries

Another area of concern to pharmaceutical physicians arises from the Medicines (Exemption from Licences) (Clinical Trials) Order[3] which requires the medical adviser to sign a certificate stating, *inter alia*, that he has satisfied himself as to the accuracy of the summaries specified in the Order and, having regard to the contents of those summaries, is of the opinion that it is reasonable for the proposed clinical trial to be undertaken. The question arises whether the employed medical adviser might be liable in proceedings for negligence. This could arise where the medical adviser failed to exercise due care in signing for the said summaries and the clinical trial subject suffered injuries as a direct consequence of some error contained therein. Because the medical adviser was negligent when signing for the summaries, he would be personally liable on the grounds that the subject of the clinical trial must be a person he should have had in mind at the time of signing and to whom he owes a common law duty of care. It is probably normally sufficient that the doctor concerned satisfies himself or herself that appropriately qualified persons have been responsible for the range of tests carried out and for preparing the reports and summaries, and ensures that they do not disclose any obvious or apparent errors. Thus, the doctor's obligation in relation to the summaries is to certify that they are accurate, which means that they do not in any way distort or corrupt the effect of the material which has been summarised. The doctor must also certify, having regard to those summaries, that it is reasonable to undertake the proposed trial. In both cases, the medical adviser's duty of care is that of the skilled medical practitioner having professional experience in the conduct of clinical trials.

The relationship of employment imposes a duty on the employer to indemnify the employee against all expenses, losses and liabilities incurred in the reasonable performance of his employment. This may extend to negligent acts or omissions, but whether it would extend to certification of summaries would depend upon the particular circumstances. It would probably be advisable for individual medical advisers to discuss the extent of the indemnity which their employer would be prepared to provide. It might be as well to bring specifically to the notice of the employer the specific duty imposed by certifying clinical trial material. In theory, an employer can take action against an employee to recoup his losses. An employee has a duty to take reasonable care in his work; if the employer has to pay damages because he did not, the employer could recover an indemnity from his employee. This would probably not happen. In theory, an insurer providing cover to the employer could bring a claim against an employee; in practice, however, there is a 'gentleman's agreement' amongst nearly all insurance companies engaged in employers' liability insurance not to make claims for insurance against employees, except in cases of collusion or wilful misconduct. It would seem that an employee would probably not be exposed to personal liability in the normal course of events. The employer would be sued, the insurer would handle the action and pay the relevant compensation—and that would be the end of the matter. However, as the employee might have a theoretical liability, for example, where the employer pays without insurance and seeks recovery from the employee, it would be prudent for the medical adviser to take out his own insurance or confirm that the employer has adequate insurance cover for the medical adviser as an individual. As stated above, a plaintiff who felt that a specific employee was particularly responsible for the event complained of might well join the employee in his action against the employer.

It should be noted that the accurate signing of summaries is but one of the many duties undertaken by a pharmaceutical physician which, if undertaken negligently, could lead to him being personally liable.

## Unlicensed medicines

Medicines can be supplied even if not licensed when they are wanted by doctors for particular named patients, but some of the requests received may give pause for thought. The product may have been licensed in the past but discontinued for some reason. It may have been in the research and development stage, but a decision was taken not to market it, or it may have been taken off the market because problems had arisen. On the other hand, patients may need these products or be likely to benefit from them. Clearly, a judgement has to be made, and a pharmaceutical physician would doubtless be at the forefront here. It is not a matter upon which any helpful advice can be given. Each company knows its own products best and has to make its own decision.*

## Fraud and misconduct in clinical trials

Finally, there is the question of fraud and misconduct in clinical trials—thinking here of the situation in which the investigator commits some sort of fraud or misconduct while carrying out a trial. This may be as basic as simply making up the results. Fraud and irregularity are most likely to be avoided if there is strict adherence to the principles of good clinical research. Familiarity with these is essential for investigators, who must both be aware that monitoring and audit procedures will be carried out and understand what these mean.

There has perhaps been a tendency in the past to take no positive action when a company has found some form of misconduct in a clinical trial. It has terminated the particular investigator's work and discarded the results—but nothing else. This attitude is no longer tenable.

*Further discussion of this matter appears in Chapter 8 of this book.

If a company suspects or determines that there is a problem of this nature, it must take appropriate action. The ABPI is at present investigating how this might best be done, as care must be taken not to be accused of libel without having any evidence to rebut the allegation. The ABPI would also like to hear about such matters and in appropriate circumstances would be prepared to make complaints itself to the General Medical Council (which, in fact, it has done already). This is an issue in which the ABPI is taking a particular interest at the present time, with a view to assisting the industry to do all it can to stamp out unacceptable behaviour. Clearly, it is an area where the pharmaceutical physician working in the company responsible for the clinical trials holds a pivotal position. He and his staff are best placed to detect any evidence of fraud or misconduct.

## Common sense

Common sense sometimes seems to be conspicuously absent where matters touching legal requirements are concerned. Anyone who reads the *New Scientist* may have learnt about the actions of a chemical company in relation to the hazard warning data sheets (not to be confused with Medicines Act data sheets) which have to be supplied to those who handle or use potentially hazardous substances, and which have been the subject of advice from the ABPI. Although companies may be *asked* for them on all their products, they are in fact *needed* only where they may be a hazard to those who handle them because they are corrosive, inflammable or dangerous in some other way. The particular case referred to in the *New Scientist* concerned a hazard warning data sheet to accompany distilled water. It set out in full the problems and the remedies. The recommendation in the hazardous situation where distilled water was spilt on someone's hands was to wash it off quickly with soap and water!

## References

1. The Code of Practice for the Pharmaceutical Industry (The Association of the British Pharmaceutical Industry—January 1991).
2. The Medicines (Advertising to Medical and Dental Practitioners) Regulations 1978 (SI 1978 no 1020) H.M.S.O.
3. The Medicines (Exemption from Licences) (Clinical Trials) Order 1981 (SI 1981 no 164) H.M.S.O.

## DISCUSSION
**Dr D. Burley**: Do you see any anomaly in the fact that a pharmaceutical physician in his errors of judgement is subject to criminal law,

whereas for other members of the medical profession it is a matter for civil law and they are well supported by their defence union? Would the ABPI like to set up a defence scheme for pharmaceutical physicians?

**Mr Massam**: I think this will not arise in the ordinary course of events. In the one case where it did, there were probably unusual circumstances. There are a few actions which are clearly offences. It is not a very high risk, although the Medicines Control Agency may have other views.

**Dr J.K. Dewhurst**: With regard to the use of unlicensed medication on a named patient basis, I understand that the patient need not be named so long as the physician is making a request for a specific patient.

**Mr Massam**: There is no legal requirement for the company to know the patient's name, although a lot of companies do like to know, particularly if it is a rather difficult request to agree to. Of course, most requests for unlicensed medicines are for different strengths of existing medicines and do not present a problem. There may be no pharmaceutical form of a particular medicine suitable for children, a suitable unlicensed dose form is made, and there is no question of patients' names in such cases. However, if somebody wanted to use thalidomide, for example, the company would want to know the name of the patient.

**Dr P.I. Adnitt**: Is a distinction made in law, particularly under the Consumer Protection Act, between *supplying* and *selling* an unlicensed medicine on request?

**Mr Massam**: It makes no difference, as far as I am aware. A judgement has to be made with a difficult substance.

**Dr K.M. O'Sullivan**: Mr Massam invited us to use common sense in what we do, but on many occasions judgements handed down both by the courts and by other organisations seem to lack it. We have to try to outguess the non-commonsensical judgements that may be made, and it can be difficult sometimes to proceed on the basis of common sense.

**Mr Massam**: Of course the judge has to take the law as he finds it, not as he would like to find it. I think a little common sense would help, but I do not lay it down as a legal principle.

# 3 | Legal responsibilities of pharmaceutical physicians: view of the Medicines Control Agency

**James P. Canlin**
*Barrister, Assistant Solicitor, Department of Health*

## Introduction

Although this chapter is stated to be a Medicines Control Agency (MCA) viewpoint, the views expressed herein are mine and not those of the MCA or of the Department of Health of which the MCA is a part, or indeed of any other government department.

## The Medicines Act 1968

The Medicines Act 1968, and the system of licensing of medicinal products which it introduced, was the direct result of the thalidomide tragedy. The purpose, which runs through the whole of the legislation, is simple. Broadly stated, it is to secure that, so far as is humanly possible, medicinal products are not made available to patients unless safe, of adequate quality, and efficacious. The Medicines Act makes provision for a number of different kinds of licence, including a manufacturer's licence, required by anyone wishing to manufacture or assemble a medicinal product, and a wholesale dealer's licence which must be obtained by anyone wishing to be a wholesaler of medicinal products. But perhaps the most important licence is the product licence. My remarks will be directed primarily to this licence, though many of the points will be relevant to the other types of licence.

It is against the background of the broad purpose of the Medicines Act that I will consider the legal responsibilities of pharmaceutical physicians.

By Section 7 of the Medicines Act, no person shall sell, supply or export; or procure the sale, supply or exportation*; or procure the

---

*It should however be noted that, pursuant to S48 of the Act, the restrictions in Section 7 and Section 8 of the Act relating to exportation have been 'postponed' and the Sections should be read as though references to exportation were omitted.

manufacture or assembly of any medicinal product except in accordance with a product licence. Equally, no person shall import a medicinal product except in accordance with such a licence. That general statement is, inevitably, subject to several exemptions. An important exemption is that provided by Section 9 which disapplies the provisions of Sections 7 and 8 to anything done by a doctor or dentist which relates to a medicinal product specially prepared or imported by him or to his order for administration to a particular patient of his, the so-called 'named-patient' exemption. Another exemption is provided by Section 10 in favour of pharmacists which, among other things, enables them to prepare or dispense a medicinal product in accordance with a prescription of a medical practitioner.

The responsibility for licensing medicinal products is placed by the Act upon the licensing authority, which is defined in Section 6 as those Ministers concerned with health and agriculture in the several parts of the United Kingdom, acting jointly or severally. The Act is also concerned with veterinary medicinal products, but I propose to ignore those products. The Authority is advised by civil servants in the MCA who include members of the appropriate specialties, and by the Medicines Commission and the committees established under Section 4 of the Medicines Act, of which the best known is perhaps the Committee on the Safety of Medicines. The details of how applications for licences are considered and determined are beyond my remit, but I would just mention the important point that an application may not be refused unless the advice of the appropriate committee or, if there is no such committee, of the Commission has first been taken.

## Product licence

An applicant for a product licence must submit with his application the material specified in Regulation 4 of, and Schedule 1 to, the Medicines (Applications for Product Licences and Clinical Trial and Animal Test Certificates) Regulations 1971 (S.I. 1971/973). That is a lengthy schedule. In addition to such obvious matters as the name and address of the applicant, the required information includes details of the active ingredients, indications for use, description of the method of manufacture, copies of reports of any experimental and biological studies, and so on. There is also a European dimension in that Article 4 of Directive 65/65/EEC on the approximation of provisions laid down by law, regulation or administrative action relating to medicinal products also prescribes what particulars and documents must accompany an application for what is there called a 'product authorisation'. In most, if not all, cases the pharmaceutical physician will be closely involved in

the work leading up to the preparation of, and in preparing, much of
that material for submission with the application. Further, all licences
must be renewed periodically, usually at intervals of five years, and an
application for renewal must be accompanied by prescribed particulars. Here, too, the pharmaceutical physician will be involved.

What are the pharmaceutical physician's legal responsibilities in this
context? The legislation does not place any responsibilities directly on
anyone other than the applicant for a licence or, where a licence has
been granted, the licence holder. In the great majority of cases this will
be a company or other corporate body of whom the physician will be an
employee or, where he is an independent consultant, a client of his. Any
legal liability, therefore, whether criminal or civil, will be that of the
applicant company and not of any employee or consultant of that
company, even though he may have been directly responsible for the
act giving rise to the liability.

## Criminal law

Section 45 of the Act makes it an offence for, among other things, an
applicant for a licence to give false information in connection with that
application. On the face of it, therefore, it will be the company, and not
any of its employees or consultants, who will be liable under that
section. But it should be noted that Section 124 provides that where an
offence committed by a body corporate is proved to have been committed with the consent and connivance of, or to be attributable to any
neglect on the part of any director, manager, secretary or other similar
officer of the corporation, he, too, is liable. Again, though, this will not
catch the ordinary employee, however eminent his position in the
company. Still less will it catch a consultant, who of course is not an
employee. What is not clear from the legislation is whether the consent,
connivance etc must be by the director etc acting as such or whether it is
sufficient that the individual just happens to be a director though at the
time of the consent or connivance he was acting in some other capacity.
My own view is that, given that penal provisions in statutes are to be
construed narrowly, the former view would prevail, although I suspect
that in practice it might not matter very much and that each case would
depend on its own facts.

However, apart from the statutory offences created by Sections 45
and 124, an employee or consultant who, for example, deliberately
falsifies data submitted in connection with an application for a licence
could attract criminal liability under the general law. Such an act
might well amount to the offence of forgery or conspiracy although,

here too, in any given case it would depend very much upon the particular facts.

## Civil law

Just as the Act places primary responsibility for any offences committed under it on the applicant for a licence or the licence holder so too in practice will any civil liability fall. The Act does not concern itself with civil liability as such. The sanctions for breaches of its provisions are primarily criminal but, if need be, the civil remedy of injunction would be available if the criminal sanction proved inadequate. Civil liability may of course arise in relation to a third party who suffers injury through being treated with a medicinal product. The claim would normally be brought in negligence against the manufacturer or distributor. This is because it will be unusual for there to be a direct contractual relationship between the manufacturer or supplier and the patient. In the great majority of cases the manufacturer or supplier will be a body corporate which is incapable of negligence itself since it is purely a legal entity with no physical or mental capabilities of its own. Whatever it does it must do by its officers and employees. Any negligence therefore, if negligence there be, in relation to a harmful medicinal product will be that of one or more of those responsible for its development, manufacture and marketing. However, although a pharmaceutical physician will normally be liable for any negligent act or omission of his, just as any of us are, where that act or omission occurs in the course of his employment the doctrine of vicarious liability will operate to render his employer liable; in other words, his negligence will be imputed to the employer even if that employer is a company and thus incapable itself of any negligent act.

I would expect that, in the usual way, the injured party would choose to proceed against the employer to the exclusion of, though possibly in addition to, the primary tortfeasor,* simply because the employer will normally be better placed to meet any award of damages that may be given. Also, it is unlikely that someone who claims to have suffered injury as the result of a defective medicinal product would, initially at least, know the identities of the individuals who had participated in its development. The position of a consultant is somewhat different because he, of course, is not an employee and therefore the doctrine of vicarious liability would have no application. But again, and for the same reason, I would expect that an injured party would be more likely

---

*A person guilty of breach of duty leading to liability for damages.

to proceed against the person or body responsible for marketing the product. Unless the licensing authority or one of its advisory bodies was alleged to be liable also, as happened in the Opren and Factor VIII cases, it would have no direct interest in such proceedings, though naturally it would be interested because of its continuing regulatory functions after a licence has been granted.

For these reasons, it is unlikely that a pharmaceutical physician would in practice find himself a defendant in civil proceedings at the suit of a party claiming to have been injured as the result of taking a medicinal product in the development or manufacture of which that practitioner had played a part, though the possibility is there in theory.

Nevertheless, that is not the end of the story. A pharmaceutical physician engaged in the development etc of medicinal products, whether as an employee or as a consultant, will owe certain legal duties to his employer or client which may be expressed as a duty to perform those things which he is employed or retained to do efficiently and with due care. It may be that, as a result of some act or omission in the course of his employment, he breaches one or more of those duties, which might render him liable to dismissal and/or to pay damages. This, too, would not be a matter with which the licensing authority would be concerned.

## Regulatory authorities

The regulatory authorities (by which I mean the licensing authority and the advisory bodies) are required to look either to the applicant for a licence or to a licence holder to discharge the duties imposed by the Act. In so doing, I think they would expect, to the extent that those duties can only be performed on behalf of the applicant or licence holder by its officers or employees, that the applicant or licence holder will seek to employ only those who are competent to perform them to a professional standard and in a professional manner. In other words, the pharmaceutical physician, and indeed anyone else engaged in this field, will in all respects act in the way expected of any professional: that he acknowledges a duty to those other than his immediate employer or client who might be affected by his actions. Thus, in carrying out its licensing function the licensing authority would expect both to be appraised of all information relevant to that function whether or not that information is favourable or unfavourable to the applicant, and also that in carrying out research or other work in connection with an application for a licence proper professional standards would be observed.

It will be seen, *vis-à-vis* the pharmaceutical physician and the regulatory authorities, that the question is not so much one of general law but of professional ethics, and (again emphasising that it is my personal view) that a physician who measures up to the standards demanded of his profession has little to fear from the regulatory authorities.

**Summary**

My view of the matter is that the pharmaceutical physician will not normally be subject to any direct legal responsibilities under the provisions of the Medicines Act and the other legislation relating to the regulation of medicinal products, but that any such physician engaged in the development and licensing* of such a product will have responsibilities both under civil and possibly criminal law by reason of his professional relationship with the applicant for a licence or licence holder.

**DISCUSSION**
**Dr D. Burley**: Both Mr Massam and Mr Canlin mentioned thalidomide in the context of an unlicensed medicine. There is no doubt that thalidomide is now a very valuable drug in certain areas. It is life-saving in erythema nodosum leprosum and valuable in Behçet's syndrome and actinic prurigo. It is also under investigation for the treatment of graft-host rejection. The problem is not that it is an unlicensed medicine, but how to find a supplier. Chemie Grunenthal, who originally marketed the drug in 1957, are unwilling to supply it to any country without some sort of indemnity against accidental misuse from the local medicines control agency, which I believe the UK MCA is unwilling to give.

**Mr Canlin**: I doubt whether the MCA has any power to give such an indemnity.

**Prof J. Thomson**: Mr Massam mentioned the duties of the doctor in signing forms in respect of promotional material and proposed clinical trials. If there is a breach of these provisions, is it criminal or civil liability?

---

*The exposure of the physician to civil liability in cases where unlicensed medicines, or licensed medicines intended for use for unlicensed indications, are prescribed is separately examined in Chapter 8 of this book.

**Mr Massam**: The clauses in the Code of Practice which relate to claims and comparisons are much the same as in the Regulations [the Medicines (Advertising to Medical and Dental Practitioners) Regulations 1978]. Therefore, when an individual gives a certification he is in fact saying that in his opinion the advertisement is consistent with the code, the regulations and the product licence—that is, a certificate which covers some matters which are subject to criminal proceedings and some which are not. There was a prosecution a few years ago when a doctor, I think the expression was 'connived at the publication of misleading information' (connived in this sense meaning 'went along with'). There is a criminal law possibility, but I hope that the MCA would not prosecute unless it was a severe case, with culpability on the part of a particular individual.

**Prof D. Lawson**: In my view, it is the duty of the pharmaceutical physician to bring to the attention of the licensing authority all relevant facts known to the company relating to an application for a product licence. Wearing my hat as an adviser to the licensing authority, it is of concern to me that this does not always happen. What is the position legally if the pharmaceutical physician fails to do this?

**Mr Canlin**: I think he would potentially be criminally liable if he knows that the relevant information has not been passed on. It would depend upon the particular facts of the case, but it could conceivably amount to conspiracy to suppress information with a view to obtaining a licence. Of course, if false information is supplied by a director or officer of the company, he would be caught by Section 124 and be personally liable as well as the company.

# 4 | Consent and information: Research on healthy volunteers and patients

**Ian Kennedy**
*Professor of Medical Law and Ethics, King's College, London*

## Introduction

My brief is very specific. It is to talk about questions of consent, I suppose because consent is thought to be one of the most important and problematical factors in the process of conducting research on people with a view to developing pharmaceutical products. This is not to say that consent is the only problem, merely that it stands out in the range of problems and difficulties which those involved in research have to confront.

## Ethics committees

Researchers are increasingly aware that the device being held up as appropriate for regulating and monitoring research on people is what has come to be called the ethics committee (on which I have distinct views, which perhaps can be aired at a different time). I think the institution of the ethics committee is an example of the government not wanting to get into the process of regulating too closely the conduct of research, and certainly wanting to avoid legislation. Instead, some gatekeeper is established, the ethics committee, to be constructed on a voluntary basis and consisting largely of, as it were, admirable amateurs who are asked to take on a host of functions, some of which are regulatory in nature, although they are passed off as not being so.

I see the development of ethics committees as manna from heaven for a government unwilling to enter this field, and disastrous in terms of those trying to conduct research, having regard to the responsibilities, the competence, the range of skills, and the delays associated with them. Be that as it may, the monitoring of the proper obtaining of consent is seen as one of the central issues in the conduct of research with which ethics committees should be concerned, and consequently one of their primary responsibilities. It is, therefore, one of the issues with which those engaged in the conduct of research have to be concerned because they have to satisfy the ethics committee, whether it is one attached to a local district health authority or created by industry 'in-house'.

## Importance and validity of consent

How does the researcher meet the demands of the responsible ethics committee as regards consent? Let us begin by asking a simple question: why is consent given so much importance? The simple answer is that if people are being asked to volunteer, to act altruistically for others, they should ordinarily, whenever possible, be given the choice whether or not to involve themselves. Preference for the volunteer rather than the conscript is a general proposition of our society. Of course, if there is the possibility of choice (leaving aside those circumstances in which it may not be possible), there should be the ability to make a choice which is considered and reflected upon. This in turn invites the question what it is that the individual should be entitled to consider and reflect upon so as to make his choice, a choice that is valid and can be properly relied upon.

## Consent: general principles

What makes consent valid? In law and moral philosophy (they are not distinct in this area) there are three components to the notion of consent:

— the person consenting must be competent to give consent;
— the consent must be freely given;
— the consent must be appropriately informed.

*Competence*, both in matters of ethics and law, is understood in terms of comprehension, whether someone understands or is capable of understanding what is being put to him or her, and capable of making a choice. Obviously, there are problems about competence as regards children, the mentally ill, the mentally retarded or those who are now described as having learning difficulties, and the senile.

Consent has to be given voluntarily or freely. In discussing what this means, any idea of forcible gaining of consent can be excluded. That is not how research is conducted. I am concerned with rather more subtle difficulties, what the Americans with their wonderful love of descriptive phrases call 'contextual duress', a nice phrase that captures what is involved, namely, that from time to time there arise circumstances in the conduct of research in which the question has at least to be raised whether the person who is saying 'yes' really means 'no', or 'I don't know and perhaps ought to say yes'. For example, a patient may be asked by his doctor, on whom he will have to depend during his treatment. Patients are already supplicants, if not mendicants, and in such circumstances may well feel obliged to say 'yes'.

Considerable difficulties are also posed when firms use their employees as research subjects. I have heard vehement declamations in favour of doing research on employees: 'They know', it is said, 'that there are no "brownie points" associated with volunteering'; 'they know that they are doing it entirely voluntarily'. Of course, if it could be shown that they do it for other reasons having to do with the pressure they feel they are under, it would raise problems both in ethics and law. The context in which students may appear to volunteer is also of concern. The disequilibrium of power between the tutor and the student may mean that the latter says 'yes' when really he or she is equivocal on the matter. The patient, the employee, the student, together with prisoners and the military are, therefore, all classic examples which should cause the researcher at least to ask further questions. All of them are regarded as problematical in the published guidelines on research.

Lastly, consent must be based upon *appropriate information*. Of course, this begs the question of what information is appropriate. As a matter of general principle, being given appropriate information means knowing something about the risks involved, the degree of inconvenience that may be experienced, the ability to withdraw from the exercise without any sanction, the possibility of compensation if something goes wrong, and whether there will be any remuneration and, if so, what its terms are.

To those general principles let me add one further *alleged* principle, that consent is valid only if it is written. As a legal principle, this is of course not the case. Writing is evidence only of consent; it is nothing else. It tends to show that the person has consented, but, of course, if written consent is obtained without there having been appropriate information or it is obtained under duress, it is worth no more than the paper on which it is written.

That said, the best practice is undoubtedly to obtain consent in writing, if only because it is the best evidence later if someone says 'I did not know' or 'I did not agree'. It is, however, only *evidence*. As the case of *Chatterton* v. *Gerson** made clear, even if something is recorded in

*An English case involving allegations of battery and negligence against a doctor [1981] QB 432.

writing, it is not of itself proof that consent has in fact been appropriately obtained. Mr Justice Bristow stated that

> . . . getting a patient to sign a proforma expressing consent to undergo
> the operation 'the effect and nature of which have been explained to me
> . . .' should be a valuable reminder to everyone of the need for explana-
> tion and consent. But it would be no defence . . . if no explanation had in
> fact been given.

## Law and guidelines

Before expanding upon those general principles, let me first make clear
that there is no specific or special law in the UK regulating the conduct
of research on people. It is often pointed out that, while there is the most
extraordinarily complicated law regulating the conduct of research on
animals, there are no laws directed specifically at the conduct of
research on people, contrary, for example, to the position in France or
the Republic of Ireland. Therefore, in stating the law, we rely on
general principles. Thus, we can say that, as a matter of law, failure to
obtain consent may well bring criminal and civil liability on those who
may thereafter have dealt with the volunteer. Having said that, in the
UK there is no specific law that says 'you have got to do so and so, and
failure to do so will bring liability'. Law, however, may well be on the
horizon in the form of European law, since in this area (as in many
others) we will ultimately be guided by developments in Europe.

Where does this leave us? There is the general law as a guide, and
various declarations and guidelines. The first and most significant
declaration is international: the Helsinki Declaration on the conduct of
research. At a national level, there are guidelines on the conduct of
research in the UK, setting out, in particular, what is ethically appropriate in the obtaining of consent. These include the Royal College of
Physicians Guidelines, the Association of the British Pharmaceutical
Industry (ABPI) Guidelines, and the long-awaited Department of
Health Circular. In Europe, there are the Guidelines of Good Clinical
Practice for Trials of Medicinal Products.

## The European Guidelines

It is these European Guidelines which, in my view, we should concentrate on. They currently take the form of exhortation, and are to be read
together with the international and UK Codes. For those who operate
in Europe, however, they are already serving as the basis of practice,
not only because they represent a European view of what is ethically

appropriate but, more important, they will be translated into a Directive in due course, and thus ultimately become the law in this area. Thus, it is common sense to bring current practice into line with them as soon as possible.

Let us examine these European Guidelines, representing as they do current thinking about the best ethical practice and what will ultimately become law. First, good clinical practice is defined in the Guidelines as

> a standard by which clinical trials are designed, implemented and reported so that there is public assurance that the data are credible and that the rights, integrity and confidentiality of subjects are protected.

There is thus at the outset a reflection of the two-way traffic of research, that good data should be produced but only in circumstances and on terms whereby the rights of those who are volunteers are appropriately respected.

## Informed consent

The Guidelines define the term 'informed consent'—which is a very rare phenomenon; if a lawyer specialising in this area were asked to define 'informed consent' he or she may be moved to say 'How long is a piece of string?' or 'How much time do you have?'. The further one proceeds, the longer it takes because the more complicated it becomes. Here, however, the European Commission through its Guidelines states what informed consent is: 'the voluntary . . .' (notice the use of the word voluntary: although it is using the aphorism of informed consent, the definition contains the three elements of consent referred to earlier)

> . . . confirmation of a subject's willingness to participate in a particular trial, and the documentation thereof. This confirmation should only be sought after information has been given about the trial including an explanation of its objectives, potential benefits and risks and inconveniences, and of the subject's rights and responsibilities in accordance with the current revision of the Declaration of Helsinki.

Although more is left out than is included, there is much of interest here. It suggests the range of information which has to be covered: 'objectives, potential benefits and risks and inconveniences, and the subject's rights . . .', and the need to give information as well as reasserting the notion of voluntariness. By referring, however, to the Helsinki Declaration, it accepts (since the Helsinki Declaration accepts) that some research may be conducted without consent. I do not know whether this definition of informed consent takes us much further, except to provide headings to which our more particular concerns may be attached.

The *details of informed consent* are then set down in the Guidelines (Paragraphs 1.8–1.14). Without referring to them *in extenso*, I will mention some of the features of informed consent which are identified. First, it is stated that the principles in the current revision of the Helsinki Declaration should be implemented, which is curious as a starting point because the Helsinki Declaration contemplates that in certain circumstances consent may not be required. Second, the Guidelines state that information should be given in both oral and written form, which is important for those developing or designing protocols for submission to ethics committees. They would be well advised to develop standard information leaflets or protocols for presentation to ethics committees so that members of such committees can see what information a volunteer is to be given. Of course, because it is in written form, this also means that the volunteer can take it away and reflect. The Guidelines then say that a volunteer should be given ample opportunity to enquire about the details of the proposed research, and that the protocol should record that opportunity for discussion has been allowed. Next, it is made clear that consent to take part in research is good only if it is made clear that refusal to participate, or withdrawal at any stage, is allowed without disadvantage. The subject must, furthermore, be allowed sufficient time to decide.

Another most important feature of the Guidelines is that the volunteer must be given information about the procedure for compensation in case of injury; in other words, the effect of the Guidelines is that there is now a *requirement* that the sponsor of the research must have provided for compensation in case of injury, as the ABPI and other guidelines suggest.

## Requirements for consent

There are, then, at least six factors set out in the Guidelines (Paragraphs 1.8–1.12) which touch on requirements for consent:

— implementation of the Helsinki Declaration;
— oral and written information;
— ample opportunity to enquire about details;
— the right to refuse or withdraw at any stage without disadvantage;
— sufficient time to decide;
— access to information about compensation.

A seventh factor is more detailed and concerns what information must be passed on. There must be a

> full and comprehensive explanation of the study (including its aims, expected benefits for the subjects and/or others, reference treatments/placebo, risks and inconveniences—e.g. invasive procedures—and, where appropriate, an explanation of alternative, recognised standard medical therapy.

That is the first part of the European Guidelines. Whenever it becomes law it will invite a fair amount of dispute about the range of possible interpretations.

## Procedure for obtaining consent

First, a consent form must be signed and the signature dated, and the consent be appropriately recorded. It seems to be intended that the volunteer's signing is taken as confirmation that he or she understood and freely chose to take part in the research. The implication would appear to be that, by signing, the volunteer signs away, as it were, any claim later that he or she was misled. This is a rather curious provision which may need some further teasing out.

## Research on the incompetent

Lastly, there is the vexed question: 'What if the intended research subject is incompetent?' Here I would draw attention to the well-known distinction between therapeutic and non-therapeutic research. Therapeutic research is defined as that in which there is a dual intention on the part of the researcher, an intention both to care for and benefit the patient and to develop data of a generalisable nature. Non-therapeutic research is defined as that in which the researcher has only one intention, to develop data of a generalisable nature pursuant to a valid scientific theory. It is clear that the European Guidelines contemplate that only research which can properly be called therapeutic may be conducted on someone who is incompetent. Non-therapeutic research may not be carried out on the incompetent.

This may be a matter on which there will be further political debate before the European Guidelines are fully implemented. The issue raised is one of great complexity. All the documents and guidelines, whether international or national, which have so far appeared hedge their bets on whether it is ever justifiable to conduct non-therapeutic research on, for example, the senile or young children who, by reason of incompetence, cannot consent. Young children have young children's illnesses. If it is impermissible to carry out research on healthy children to discover, for example, possible variations between the healthy and the ill, progress in dealing with these illnesses will be difficult. Equally, there may be a case for non-therapeutic research on those suffering from Alzheimer's disease, when the intention is to search for clues rather than benefit the patient (but at the same time with no or minimal risk). Such research would be outlawed according to the European Guidelines because, first, non-therapeutic research is defined as research where there is no direct clinical benefit to the subject and, second, in such non-therapeutic research consent must always be given by the signature of the subject. Obviously, the volunteer cannot sign when he or she is incompetent. Thus non-therapeutic research in areas where there may be a desperate need for it to be carried out is outlawed by the European Guidelines.

By contrast, the Guidelines contemplate that, in certain circumstances, *therapeutic* research may be carried out on the incompetent. The Guidelines state that if the relevant ethics committee approves the research and if, in the view of some independent person, the research, by being also intended to be therapeutic, is in the patient-volunteer's best interests, the research may be carried out.

## Summary

This, in the briefest form, is an outline of the law and ethics relating to consent in research. I have followed as a model the European Guidelines, since not only are they intended to serve as guides for good practice but it is also intended that they should become law in due course.

## DISCUSSION

**Dr B. Gennery**: I have always assumed that the European Guidelines, like all the other Directives on pharmaceuticals (and indeed the Medicines Act) apply to pharmaceutical companies only and not to universities, so that non-therapeutic research would not be covered if it was conducted by a university.

**Prof. Kennedy**: Because the Guidelines are directed towards the conduct of clinical trials, it seems to me that they extend to anyone engaged in them.

**Mr I. Dodds-Smith**: I think the Guidelines apply, on the basis that the pharmaceutical manufacturer has to confirm that his work is being conducted in accordance with the Guidelines, whether done inside or outside his establishment.

**Dr J.L. Bem**: Can written consent for studying children ever be valid in law? Can a parent ever be legally entitled to take a risk of injury or death on behalf of a child by volunteering that child?

**Prof. Kennedy**: English law is relatively clear. While the UK guidelines are somewhat equivocal, the European Guidelines seem to have no hesitation in affirming that where the research involves dual intentions, for example, if a child has leukaemia and there are treatments (a), (b) and (c), none of which seems to be better than the others and all of which merit some kind of randomised controlled experiment, given the risk of the child otherwise dying, it would be legitimate to put the child into one of those cohorts, provided that it would not suffer adversely in any way. The European document makes clear that if the child is not ill, or if the child is ill but the research is for something other than the care of its illness, unless the child is competent to make a decision for itself (English law would probably say it would be very rare for a child to be deemed competent until adulthood), the parent may not consent on its behalf or, if he purports to consent, the consent would be invalid.

**Dr Bem**: It would perhaps be better to advise parents not to consent to a therapeutic trial because it might be very stressful if something happened after they had signed consent, or perhaps it might be better not to tell the parent all that may be involved.

**Prof. Kennedy**: I take the opposite view on the latter point. In law, and I think also in ethics, the notion of what is sometimes called the therapeutic privilege (that people are not told what is happening because it may adversely affect their recovery or whether they want to have the treatment) cannot apply in the case of a parent or a legal guardian of a child. The parent needs to be able to weigh all the factors, so there is an obligation to give all the relevant information. It may cause extra inconvenience, but I would imagine every ethics committee would be extremely careful to ensure that the process of informing the parents or the legal guardian had been carried out properly, and that the research could be shown to be therapeutic.

**Dr D. Burley**: I do not think that patient consent or agreement should be greatly different between research and ordinary medical treatment. The problem for me is how bad or frequent risks have to be before it is necessary to draw them to the attention of the patient or subject. In the Sidaway* case the decision seemed to be that a surgeon could fail to disclose a 2% hazard of a serious complication with impunity, provided the patient did not press him too hard. This would be much too high a percentage for any drug. Manufacturers have difficulties over what they should put in their literature and what may be safely omitted in terms of adverse effects.

**Prof. Kennedy**: In the context of *treatment* there are rare circumstances in which it may be defensible not to obtain consent, and the law contemplates this to be the case. The same may not be true in the case of *research*, and is certainly not the case with non-therapeutic research where the therapeutic privilege has no place.

As regards what must be drawn to a person's attention, *Sidaway* sets out the law when patients are being treated. *Sidaway*, however, has no relevance to *research* where we must begin again from first principles. When the research is therapeutic, except in the rare circumstances in which therapeutic privilege may apply, the researcher has an obligation to inform the patient that he is involved in research and set out the risks predictably associated therewith. When the research is non-therapeutic, the law limits the researcher to research which carries only a minimal risk: to expose a volunteer to more would be unlawful and unethical. The researcher must set out the range of inconveniences and risks which could arise despite the best efforts to avoid them. The aim, after all, is to empower the volunteer to make a considered choice.

**Question from the Floor**: Can Professor Kennedy comment on the advice by Lord Scarman that when a protocol is proffered to a patient from whom consent is being sought advice should also be given about possible alternative therapies?

**Prof. Kennedy**: I think Lord Scarman is correct. I always maintain that in consent to treatment, let alone consent to treatment which also involves therapeutic research, part of the information which it is obligatory in law to give to a patient, as well as the material risks which attend such intervention, is the alternative therapies — because they are as important as a description of risks in empowering someone to make a choice. The breast cancer trials, for example, are a classic example.

**Dr R. Smith**: One of the problems in obtaining consent in controlled clinical trials is telling the average patient the consequences of placebo

*\*Sidaway v. Bethlem Royal Hospital* [1985] 1All ER 643 (and see Kennedy I, *Treat me right*, Oxford University Press 1991, chapter 9).

treatment, which I think, in general, is not done well. An ethics committee has to address the issues of how an investigator will monitor potential deterioration in health and what provisions there are for rescue medication. This is very often not built into the ethical review process, maybe because many people are not aware of the risks and potential problems.

Secondly, in the revision of the Association of the British Pharmaceutical Industry Guidelines it is unfortunate that any reference to compensation because of deterioration due to placebo treatment was omitted.

**Mr Massam**: The latter point was the subject of considerable debate. Some companies were keen to have this item included, but the consensus view was to exclude it, and that is the situation at the moment. It certainly did not go by default, but was addressed in some detail.

**Prof. Kennedy**: The European Guidelines refer to placebos as being part of the information given. I regard this as a good example of the descent into detail that may have to be considered. Let us consider the notion: 'I want to conduct a randomised controlled trial'. There is no doubt that what is involved in randomisation ought to be explained: it may involve a placebo or two treatments. Then there are such issues as the possible deterioration of the patient, what are the stopping rules, and whether these should be addressed as part of the consent, bearing in mind the capacity of the volunteer to understand them. The level of detail into which we may be drawn falls within the purview of ethics committees, who should be careful to ensure that researchers have given their minds to all relevant questions. The law should not seek to spell it out in detail. If ethics committees are to do this, they will have to develop a level of sophistication previously not attained and of which I do not think most of them are capable. Furthermore, where will they find the necessary statistical, pathological, pharmacokinetic and other expertise?

**Dr R. Smith**: I agree that most ethics committees are probably not capable of reviewing this type of detail. For this reason, the pharmaceutical physician—and indeed all those working in the industry— should make sure that the principal investigator is aware of the potential risks to patients during the wash-out period *before* a trial starts, when the patients are often not seen by any physician.

**Prof. Kennedy**: This takes us slightly beyond the issue of consent, but certainly concerns the broad responsibilities of ethics committees.

**Part 2**

---

# Product liability and litigation

# 5 | Product liability issues arising out of the introduction of strict liability and procedures for dealing with multi-claimant cases

**Ian Dodds-Smith**
*Partner, McKenna & Co, Solicitors, London*

## Fault liability

The common law of negligence (which does not depend upon the existence of a contractual relationship between claimant and defendant) remains central to any discussion of product liability in the pharmaceutical field. A duty to exercise reasonable care is probably imposed on everyone who has anything to do with the supply of medicines and this paper concentrates on prescription-only medicines (rather than research products) because those are the class of medicines that have traditionally given rise to most issues of product liability. Such a duty of care is imposed not only upon the pharmaceutical company itself, but also upon the officers of the company; they can be sued in their personal capacity in respect of any negligent action or inaction on their part.[1] Likewise, the duty is imposed upon prescribing doctors and pharmacists who may become answerable for any negligence on their part.

There has been a great deal of discussion in recent years as to whether public authorities such as the regulatory authorities in this country (the licensing authority, Section 4 advisory committees and the Medicines Commission) could be sued at common law for negligence or whether they owe a duty only to the public at large rather than a duty to particular individuals. An interesting development on this matter is that in the human immunodeficiency virus (HIV) haemophilia litigation, the Court of Appeal, while not having to decide the issue given the nature of the question before them (which related to disclosure of documents), said that it felt there was a good arguable case that a duty of care *was* owed by the regulatory authorities to individual haemophiliacs injured by the use of blood products contaminated with HIV.[2] They had joined the Committee on Safety of Medicines (CSM) and other public bodies as co-defendants alongside the health authorities responsible vicariously for a number of treating physicians.

## Strict liability

Since March 1988, pharmaceutical manufacturers have been subject not only to 'fault liability' but also to strict liability pursuant to the Consumer Protection Act 1987.[3] This provides that 'producers' of products are, in principle, liable to compensate for injury caused by products that are defective in that they do not offer the level of safety that persons are entitled to expect in all the circumstances. Such liability does not replace fault liability but is an alternative basis for a claim for compensation. Strict liability is further discussed below, but an initial point to make is that, in principle, the regulatory authorities, prescribing doctors and pharmacists *do not* fall within the definition of producers, who are the focus of strict liability. There are one or two exceptions to this principle, but in general terms 'producers' means manufacturers, or importers into the European Community.[4] Strict liability therefore does not have great significance except for pharmaceutical companies themselves and not much direct significance for the medical director or any other individual within the company because he falls outside the definition of 'producer', and any claim against him must continue to be made in negligence.

## Claims experience and changes in the legal environment

As regards claims based on negligence, it is a defence to show that reasonable care has been taken. Very few product liability claims involving medicinal products have ever come to trial and none has proceeded as far as a decision on liability following full discussion of whether the duty of care has been discharged.[5] Nevertheless, most commentators believe that there has been a trend towards more exacting standards of care. This case law has not been in the area of medicines (and for that reason one must be cautious in extrapolating it), but there is a general belief that a very high standard of care will be required[6] and while the burden of proving negligence is in law left with the claimant, in practice the courts will be more ready to reverse the evidential burden of proof on to the defendant company. However, changes in the impact of the law of negligence and the introduction of strict liability are probably not the cause of the increasing flow of claims which the pharmaceutical sector has experienced. There has not only been an increase in the number of single ('one-off') claims for compensation submitted to pharmaceutical companies but also an increase in the larger 'multi-claimant' cases. The first type of claim is difficult to deal with because, regardless of the merits of the case, the costs of fighting it can quickly become out of proportion to the amount at stake—or rather the amount of an *ex gratia* payment that would settle it. Legal aid may be granted in cases which at first sight appear to have little merit, and a company that successfully defends a claim will normally have no chance to recover its costs from a legally aided claimant or the legal aid fund. Therefore, provided the company is cognisant of the risk of creating the impression that it settles every claim advanced against it, the commercial arguments in favour of settlement are often very great.

The second category of claim is the multi-claimant case that normally represents very substantial litigation. The implications in this situation are very different, and most companies view such litigation as too significant not to fight, even where the individual claims for compensation are pitched at quite a low level and the costs of defence very great. It may be asked why multi-claimant cases in respect of marketed products are now so common. The introduction of strict liability is not the reason. The cases now widely reported in the media do not involve issues of strict liability because they concern products supplied prior to March 1988. Moreover, eligibility for legal aid has dropped dramatically in the last ten years.[7] The simple answer may be that we live in a more litigious society.

Against this background some ask what will happen if contingency fees are introduced. There would not appear to be the political will to put sufficient funding into legal aid to ensure access to justice in the traditional way, which carries the safeguard that not only must the financial criteria be met but also an opinion must be forthcoming that the case has a reasonable prospect of success on its merits. Contingency fees seem to be seen as a cheap alternative by a government anxious to reduce public expenditure and are now likely to become a feature of our legal landscape.[8] This will probably increase the pressures upon pharmaceutical companies, because one of the hallmarks of a contingency fee system is arguably that the merits of the case often become less important than the identity of the putative defendant and the chance that he can be cajoled into settling a case to avoid cost, management disruption and adverse publicity.

The greater sophistication of plaintiffs' legal representation has also given a boost to this type of litigation. Some plaintiff firms are becoming more experienced in pharmaceutical matters and with the help of technical advisers are now adept at drafting a so-called generic statement of claim against a manufacturer. And how easy it is; if an adversarial position is adopted there is virtually no decision of a pharmaceutical company concerning its product, or of a licensing authority, that could not be challenged five or ten years later with a knowledge of how the literature has developed on the matters of interest. There has never been a data sheet produced with which someone will not find fault, and with the benefit of hindsight the opportunities for attack inevitably multiply greatly. Thus, it is easy to make claims, and then the media, ever vigilant for anything to do with health and litigation between patients and pharmaceutical companies that can be portrayed as a David and Goliath confrontation, will generate further interest and often more claimants. There is also increasingly an international dimension, with lawyers in different countries getting together and exchanging 'know-how' and documents, and with the press recycling the same publicity. This combination can quickly create a bandwagon effect, internationally as well as locally, with the company in question finding similar litigation surfacing worldwide.

The cost of defending such multi-claimant litigation is enormous. Such costs will not lessen with the advent of strict liability but will probably increase — not because more claims will be made but because the increased complexity of litigation (with claims advanced alternatively upon a fault and strict liability basis) is bound to be reflected in greater costs of investigation and defence. The level of damages awarded, if the claimant is successful, varies from country to country and the more well-publicised awards of US juries are, in this regard, misleading. However, the large hidden costs in terms of management time have to be taken into account as well as the legal and expert adviser costs. Defence is a labour-intensive exercise as the historical documentation alone may be colossal. In multi-claimant cases covering the greater part of the marketing period, with 10, 20 or more years of research, development and marketing, all documents relevant to the issues (always very broadly pleaded by claimants) may need to be produced. Millions of sheets of paper may therefore have to be collected, collated and reviewed before they are made available for inspection under the 'discovery' rules. In addition, reconstructing the history of marketing and the development of scientific knowledge from the international literature can be a lengthy task.

What litigation is pending at present? First, the main blood products litigation in the UK (HIV and haemophiliacs) has been settled by the government,[9] but some cases of alleged clinical negligence will proceed to trial (unless settled or discontinued in the interim) because their individual facts are viewed as unusual. There has also been considerable publicity over several thousand possible claims against Glaxo concerning its product Myodil, used as a contrast medium and alleged to have caused damage to the lining of the spinal canal.[10] Even more publicity has been generated by substantial litigation against a number of manufacturers and prescribing doctors concerning the marketing of benzodiazepines over alleged problems of dependence. It is reported that several thousand claims may be made.[11] There has also been publicity about claims relating to the marketing of intra-uterine contraceptive devices (IUCDs) and steroids, the former concerned with pelvic inflammatory disease allegedly caused by the devices, and the latter with degeneration of the muscle tissues, it is argued, caused by inappropriate long-term treatment with the products in question in the 1960s and 1970s. Most recently, it has been reported that patients are considering claims against manufacturers of human insulin, alleging that the switch from animal insulin may cause a loss of warning symptoms associated with a hypoglycaemic attack.

These claims now tend to be pursued in all UK jurisdictions. The number of claims differ, but no longer is London the only centre for product liability litigation. The impact of defending litigation in several jurisdictions at the same time cannot be underestimated bearing in mind the time that the company and its medical advisers may have to spend instructing lawyers and monitoring what is happening in each of these jurisdictions.

## The practical effect of strict liability

Against this litigious background the practical effect of strict liability for defective products will perhaps not be very radical. Strict liability was intended to make it easier for claimants to succeed in law — and the crux of the law is that the producer is liable for a defect in his product. The burden of proving the existence of an injury and a causal relationship between the defect and the injury lies with the plaintiff, but the claimant need not prove negligence on the part of the company. However, proving causation — the stumbling block in so many pharmaceutical cases — remains with strict liability. It is suggested that those who believe that a no-fault compensation scheme is a better alternative to litigation may be deluding themselves, as such schemes also require proof of causation. Most of the claims that have been brought against the industry have raised difficult issues of general causation (ie does the product cause this type of damage?) or individual causation (ie has it caused the damage in this particular case?).

The definition of a defective product under the relevant legislation is quite short: in essence, a product is defective if it does not provide the safety which a person is entitled to expect taking into account all the circumstances, which include the presentation of the product, the use to which it may reasonably be expected to be put, and the time the product was put into circulation.[12] Essentially, though, the concern is with consumer expectations and a risk/benefit analysis. This is easy to apply in cases of manufacturing or design defects, where procedures of quality control and research, respectively, have failed to disclose the existence of a defect in products leaving the manufacturer. Manufacturing defects will now be even more difficult to defend. However, the UK has adopted a defence to strict liability where the producer can show that the defect could not have been discovered given the state of technical and scientific knowledge when the product in question was supplied. This may often provide a defence to design defect allegations.[13]

The greatest practical concern arises in relation to marketing defects and, notably, the 'failure to warn' allegation. Most litigation in this area focuses upon two allegations: a failure to warn and a failure to monitor or do adequate further research after marketing has begun. In the context of marketing defects, the reference in the definition of defect to the 'presentation' of the product is crucial. What is the presentation of a product? Instructions for use and warnings are obviously key items. But in UK law 'presentation' covers all aspects of the manner in and purposes for which a product is marketed.[14] This would seem to encompass the fact that the product is supplied through an intermediary, such as a general practitioner, which leads commentators on the new law to say that the information supplied to the medical profession by the company remains relevant to the issue of whether the product is defective even though it is not directed at the patient himself. Clearly, advertisements and the activities of sales representatives relate to the 'manner' in which the product is marketed and can also potentially affect perceptions of safety. Accordingly, it would seem that deciding whether a product is defective under strict liability principles will involve a consideration of all the informational activities of the company. The importance of promotion is, of course, also reflected by the draft Advertising Directive,[15] although this Directive is quite narrow because it seems to be based upon the principle that information to doctors concerns only the issue of overtly promotional information. Technical information supplied directly to practitioners through data sheets etc is not the focus, but is clearly of as much significance from a product liability point of view as general advertising—and, of course, patient information, which is the subject of a further draft Directive.[16]

## Instructions for use and warnings

The question arises whether the advent of strict liability requires a
different approach to developing instructions for use and warnings, the
aim of which under any theory of law is to enable the user to take
reasonable steps to confront and avoid a possible danger. The doctor
can do this either by not prescribing the product to inappropriate
patients or by ensuring that sufficient information is available to the
patient regarding, for instance, the symptoms that may foreshadow an
adverse drug reaction, to ensure that any risk of injury is minimised.
There have been no reported cases in the UK on strict liability, but
there would seem to be no absolute standard for instructions for use and
warnings, and therefore the approach to their development need not
change. The major aim is to develop and maintain instructions and
warnings that reflect the changing state of knowledge and are reasonable in all the circumstances. The factors to be taken into account were
considered in a recent case in Australia concerning toxic shock syndrome allegedly caused by tampon use.[17] Having regard to this case
and other relevant case law,[18] the following may be relevant:

— the magnitude of the risk of the injury, both in terms of the
   probability of injury and its seriousness, as established by the
   literature. Where there is merely a suspicion of risk, this has to be
   weighed against the severity of the damage if the risk turns out to be
   real;
— the quality of the evidence implicating the product as a cause of
   injury. It is not safe to ignore evidence purely because it is un-
   convincing, but the quality of any studies said to provide evidence
   of hazard is important. Reports of possible hazard may properly be
   balanced against long-term and apparently safe use of the product
   in a large number of other patients;
— the information that the company has gained from adverse reaction
   monitoring and post-marketing surveillance;
— the nature of the drug and the reason for taking it—the risk/benefit
   ratio—is clearly crucial;
— the attitude of the regulatory authorities. The Australian courts, in
   the toxic shock claim, emphasised that the attitude of the regulatory
   authorities, though not decisive, is an important factor to be taken
   into account.

Patient information is now shortly to become compulsory in the
European Community.[19] We have come a long way since the late 1970s

when companies marketing oral contraceptives received letters of complaint from the Pharmaceutical Society and the Department of Health about the introduction of detailed written advice to patients in the packages of them. In ten years we have gone from a general rejection of manufacturer leaflets to a proposal in the draft Directive for patient information for over 20 heads of material—a very big change indeed. Good patient information will probably be one way (but not the only way) in which the expectation of safety can most effectively be qualified. There remains great need to explain to patients that no medical product offers absolute safety, and that the risk of adverse reaction is the price paid for effective treatment.

## Co-ordinated proceedings for multi-claimant cases

Co-ordination of proceedings merely refers to the management of a series of related claims in a manner convenient for the parties and the court. The history of this area of practice is that the early large cases—the practolol, hormone pregnancy test and pertussis vaccine litigation—were in most respects unco-ordinated. The first substantially co-ordinated proceeding in the UK involved Opren (benoxaprofen). The litigation involved over 1,000 claimants who were ultimately divided into four groups (A, B, C and D) depending in the main on the date the claims were made. A large number of claimants in group C were recently ruled out of time for bringing their proceedings.[20] This case emphasised the desirability of claimants not delaying bringing their claims. Co-ordination took place in the blood product cases and is taking place in the cases involving claims for compensation allegedly caused by Myodil and by benzodiazepines.

The most important aspect to mention regarding co-ordination is that, in principle, it is consensual—people cannot be forced into co-ordinated proceedings. In practice, those representing claimants tend to join together in a group and elect a steering committee which allocates discrete areas of the preparation and management of the litigation to the committee members, with the majority of solicitors in the group merely being responsible for individual claims. A first step is (or should be) to serve properly pleaded claims upon the defendant(s) but this will be preceded by the investigation needed to justify the grant of legal aid, where appropriate. The courts have made it clear that if they are to be able to deal effectively with this type of multi-claimant litigation, a novel framework must be devised with the help of the parties. To date, this has been done on an *ad hoc* basis, with the courts and parties learning from experience gained in similar previous litigation.[21] The major cases have tended to involve the nomination of a single judge to deal with pre-trial procedures. There is no guarantee of having the same judge for the trial, although there is an expectation that this will occur.

If litigation involves a number of potential defendants and products, a somewhat strange situation may develop. The judge seeks to set a framework for the litigation, but very often those representing the plaintiffs commence the litigation while claims are being processed for legal aid and therefore without knowing the identity of all possible defendants or even the products involved. This has certainly been the case with both the HIV and the benzodiazepine litigation. The establishment of a framework for co-ordinated litigation *before* all the defendants are known is curious; by definition, other defendants may enter the co-ordinated proceedings later and, on the face of it, have a structure imposed on them without being heard on the issues involved. In principle, they can object, but it is difficult to disturb a string of court orders establishing a procedural framework without compelling reasons.

Most co-ordinated proceedings have pleadings on generic issues and separate, individual statements of claim which adopt such parts of the master pleadings as appear appropriate, given the particular facts of the individual claims. In practice, claimants have tended to serve the 'generic statement of claim' before the individual claims, partly to answer the defendants' requests for clarification of the allegations and partly to bring pressure to bear upon the defendants to show their own hand on the issues involved. However, a master pleading is in fact merely a vehicle for setting out those parts of a claim that may be common to a large number of individual actions and can be conveniently adopted by such actions — it has no life of its own. At some point, a series of actions will be selected as vehicles to determine the various issues that arise. These issues need to be carefully considered by reference to the nature of the totality of the cases, as the aim is to ensure that the decisions in the 'lead cases' will provide a clear indication to all concerned of how the rest of the cases would fare if taken to trial. However, in pharmaceutical litigation there is rarely a common issue that, once tried, will automatically determine the outcome of the proceedings as a whole. This will perhaps be the case if there is an issue of general causation (such as arose in the pertussis litigation), and a decision in the defendants' favour should dispose of the litigation as a whole. However, questions of negligence and individual causation present a variety of issues and sub-issues, the complexion of which changes from year to year during the history of marketing as the state of scientific knowledge changes. The decision in any given case will therefore tend to turn on its own peculiar facts.

Moreover, where allegations of negligence are made, much depends upon the involvement of the prescribing doctor in the history of treatment. There is little point in looking at the issue of whether a data sheet or other corporate information provided acceptable prescribing information unless it is established that the doctor in question relied upon it. In the Australian toxic shock case, the plaintiff's claim failed because no evidence was presented that any failure to warn had any effect on the way the doctor had dealt with the plaintiff's case. These are problems inherent in pharmaceutical litigation, and have made it a poor candidate for any form of 'class action' even in the USA where class action procedures are well developed. However, in multi-claimant cases one frequently finds that the factual features of a significant number of cases are not materially different and it is possible to choose lead actions in a way that provides the court with an opportunity to give guidance on the legal importance of these individual aspects.

## Costs and cost-sharing

In multi-claimant cases, all the cases are rarely prepared and ready to proceed when the judge is first appointed. Indeed, the publicity generated by the announcement of the proceedings (often carefully promoted by the plaintiffs and their advisers) serves to increase the number of claimants, particularly where the product was widely used and the allegations of injury broad rather than discrete. In the Opren, HIV/blood product and benzodiazepine litigation, the court has decided to establish a 'cut-off date' after which claims will not be considered as part of the first group of co-ordinated proceedings. On the face of it, subject to limitation issues, there may be merits in not incurring the costs of joining this first group if the second group will be large enough to sustain any separate litigation necessary, and if membership causes no financial exposure or risk to the viability of a claim. In co-ordinated proceedings there are normally cost-sharing arrangements for plaintiffs covered by orders of the court. This takes account of the decision of the Court of Appeal in the Opren litigation that non-legally aided claimants could not ride on the back of legally-aided claims and must contribute to the costs. Claimants may feel comfortable waiting for the outcome of the lead cases from the first group rather than commit themselves to the costs of the proceedings. On the other hand, the more claimants that can be brought within the first group, the more the risk on costs (for those not legally-aided) will be spread.

In general, the courts seem keen to 'corral' as many cases as possible, in the hope that the lead cases can be chosen having regard to all the possible issues that may arise in the cases. In addition, there are questions of limitation to consider—many claimants who stood on the side-lines of the initial Opren litigation were later judged to have claims that were statute-barred. In the benzodiazepine litigation the court warned patients in strong terms of the risks of delaying making a claim and thereby falling outside the co-ordinated proceedings.[22] In any event, the concern to publicise the existence of the co-ordinated proceedings produces the somewhat unusual picture of the court asking claimants to come forward. In such circumstances, the plaintiff's advisers hardly need to advertise for clients, although isolated instances of this generated considerable adverse comment in the benzodiazepine litigation.

## Lead cases

Selection of lead cases usually results in a stay of the balance of the cases pending trial of the lead cases. None of these multi-claimant cases has proceeded to a full trial in England yet, and it is difficult to see how the lead case procedure will work out in practice. We learn as we go along. If the plaintiffs lose those lead cases, both for legal and practical funding (legal aid) reasons, the position of other claimants is poor, although in principle the cases do not create a binding precedent for any of the other cases. Equally, a defendant who loses lead cases can expect little respite from either the plaintiffs or the press. So the lead cases are all-important, and their selection and preparation will be crucial to all parties if the aim of co-ordination is to be achieved.

## References and Notes

1.  In cases begun in England in the mid-1980s concerning the marketing of Opren (benoxaprofen) the plaintiffs sued not only various members of the Eli Lilly Group of Companies but also an individual doctor having medical and research responsibility at various times.
2.  Re HIV Haemophiliac Litigation (1990) *Independent*, 2 October, Court of Appeal.
3.  The Consumer Protection Act implements the provisions of an EC Directive; see 85/374/EEC on the approximation of the laws, regulations and administrative provisions of the Member States concerning liability for defective products. OJ L210/29.
4.  See Consumer Protection Act 1987 Section 1(2).
5.  Claims in the 1970s concerning Distaval (thalidomide) marketed by Distillers, and claims arising out of the marketing of Eraldin (practolol) by ICI were settled by compensation schemes. Cases concerning alleged

adverse reactions to use of prednisolone brought against Glaxo and others were reported in 1987 as having been settled immediately prior to trial. Certain co-ordinated proceedings commenced against Eli Lilly and others in the mid-1980s relating to the marketing of Opren (benoxaprofen) were settled prior to trial. Claims against Schering Chemicals Limited concerning allegations that their hormone pregnancy test Primodos had caused teratogenic effects were discontinued by the plaintiffs with the leave of the Court in 1982 on the basis that following exchange of expert evidence there was no real possibility of the plaintiffs establishing that the products were capable of causing the alleged injuries. In *Loveday v. Renton* (1988) *Times*, 31 March, the Court found that the plaintiffs had failed to establish a causal relationship between the use of pertussis vaccine, marketed by the Wellcome Foundation and others, and brain damage in young children.

6. See for instance *Vacwell Engineering Co Ltd v. BDH Chemicals Ltd* [1971] 1 QB 88, *Devilez v. Boots Pure Drug Co Ltd* (1962) 106 Sol Jo 552.

7. There was a drop in legal aid eligibility between 1979 and 1989 from 73% to 63% of the population; see Eligibility for Civil Legal Aid: A Consultation Paper, June 1991.

8. Section 58 of the Courts and Legal Services Act 1990 allows solicitors to make conditional fee arrangements under which the solicitor will recover his normal fees and an uplift where he wins the case and nothing further if he loses. Section 58 is not yet in force as the percentage uplift is to be regulated by the Lord Chancellor and agreement on this point has not been reached. Such a fee arrangement is not to be equated with the traditional contingency fee arrangement in the United States where lawyers may recover a percentage of their clients' damages in a successful case. However, cases involving potentially low damage awards, even if they are successful, are unlikely to be attractive to those interested in conducting a claim on a contingency fee basis under Section 58 as they will wish to be sure that the likely damages are sufficient to cover an appropriate uplift where the claim is successful.

9. See *Re HIV Haemophiliac Litigation*; Ognall J, QBD 10 June 1991.

10. See *Chrzanowska v. Glaxo Laboratories Ltd* (1990) *Times*, 16 March.

11. A cut-off date of 20 September 1991 for legal aid applications for claims to be included in the existing co-ordinated proceedings was ordered in July (see *In Re Benzodiazepine Litigation*; Kennedy J, QBD 4 July 1991.)

12. Consumer Protection Act 1987 Section 3(1).

13. Consumer Protection Act 1987 Section 3(1). However, the UK has not followed precisely the wording of the relevant defence in the Directive. Section 4(1)(e) provides that it is a defence to show 'that the state of scientific and technical knowledge at the relevant time was not such that a producer of products of the same description as the product in question might be expected to have discovered the defect if it had existed in his products while they were under his control'. This seems to allow evidence of standards of testing in the industry as a whole and the economic plausibility of discovering defects to be taken into account rather than merely determining whether scientific methods existed at the relevant time that were capable of discovering the defect however time-consuming and expensive this might have been. Enforcement proceedings have been

threatened by the European Commission against HM Government for non-implementation of the Directive's terms. In this connection it is important to note that the fact of licensing is not a defence to strict liability unless the defect arises through a mandatory requirement imposed by the licensing authority such as a particular form of warning (see Section 4(1)(a)).

14. See Consumer Protection Act 1987 Section 3(2)(a).
15. Proposal for a Council Directive on advertising of medicinal products for human use (90/c 163/12: Official Journal 4.7.90).
16. Proposal for a Council Directive on the labelling of medicinal products for human use and package leaflets (90/C 58/OS: Official Journal 8.3.90).
17. *Thompson v. Johnson and Johnson Pty Ltd v. Anon* (1991) Aust. Torts Reports 81-075.
18. See in particular *Buchan v. Ortho Pharmaceutical (Canada) Ltd* (1984) 46 OR (2d) 113 which while not an English decision but a Canadian one provides some discussion on the subject.
19. Council Directive 98/341/EEC of 3 May 1989 amending Directives 65/65/EEC, 75/318/EEC and 75/319/EEC on the approximation of provisions laid down by law regulation or administrative action relating to proprietary medicinal products (Official Journal: 25.5.89).
20. *Nash and others v. Eli Lilly & Company and others* (1991) *Times*, 13 February.
21. A Guide for Use in Group Actions has now been published by the Supreme Court Procedure Committee (May 1991).
22. *In Re Benzodiazepine Litigation* QBD 4 July 1991.

## DISCUSSION

**Dr D.B. Galloway**: Mr Dodds-Smith rightly said that there is no absolute standard for product information. Might the old clinical pharmacology adage of indication, contra-indication, mode of action and adverse effects, with an appropriate balance, provide adequate information for both patient and doctor? Many of us in the pharmaceutical industry would hesitate about the kind of patient package inserts for patients in the USA, with several pages of text listing every possible option for every formulation of a product, whether or not appropriate.

**Mr Dodds-Smith**: It is easy to work out what the headings of drug information should be. The proposed patient leaflet at European level involves about 24 headings or subheadings. The difficulty, alluded to earlier, is that it is easy to say 'describe adverse reactions', but what does that mean? What should be done about extremely rare adverse reactions or about suspicions of possible harm and anecdotal case reports? Our American colleagues include everything in every document for fear of product liability. The level of suspicion properly required to justify a warning in information to doctors—let alone patients—has not been much debated in the USA.

I can perhaps best illustrate my concern by saying that the Department of Health guidelines in the UK on the production of data sheets still state that the side-effects to be mentioned in the data sheet are those most likely to be encountered in clinical practice, whereas the European Directive for patient information appears to require a fuller description of the 'undesirable effects which can occur under normal use', and a statement about the magnitude of risks with an indication, if possible, of their importance and, if necessary, the action to be taken when they occur. Where the medicinal product is new, the patient is to be expressly invited to communicate to his doctor or pharmacist any undesirable effect not mentioned in the leaflet.

There are no absolute standards concerning warnings and I believe companies are rightly concerned about the implications of selectivity, yet the tradition in this country, even in relation to data sheets, is that companies do not set out for doctors a text book on every drug. I do not know at the moment where the debate will lead, but at Community level patient information remains a separate and primary focus of information about medicines.

**Dr O'Sullivan**: The product liability claims in relation to HIV and acquired immune deficiency syndrome (AIDS) will be based on the manufacturers being held responsible for a disease unidentified at the time their products were used. How can a company be held responsible for such action?

**Mr Dodds-Smith**: In relation to the HIV haemophiliac litigation, the general policy in the UK was not to sue the companies but rather the health authorities and clinicians—a decision I think related to the difficulty of determining in any individual case from which product seroconversion resulted and when. The UK does not have the US 'market share concept' of liability which applies when the identity of the allegedly defective product is not clear. The discoverability issue would have been important if cases had been brought against the companies. Under fault liability (which would have governed these claims because strict liability under the Consumer Protection Act is not retrospective) a company is not liable if it has taken reasonable steps to discover the hazard. In contrast, under strict liability, the focus is the quality of the product, and patients are normally entitled to compensation for injury caused by the defect. This created a big problem in the UK because the government accepted the need for a 'state of the art' defence against strict liability, which amounts to saying that the product is defective but the manufacturer should have a defence because in the existing state of scientific and technological knowledge the defect could not have been discovered. The European Economic Community (EEC) Directive allows such a defence at the option of each Member State. On this basis, a person will not be responsible for unknown defects. A difficulty of interpretation that remains is the amount of effort that may be expected to be made to discover a problem. In other jurisdictions (America and Australia) it has been argued by plaintiffs that companies could have done more in relation to the risk of HIV, that because blood products were known to transmit viruses, viz hepatitis, they could have heat-treated earlier—illustrating the point that plaintiffs will always argue about whether or not something was discoverable or avoidable.

**Mr R. Goldberg**: A number of writers in the strict liability area have argued that because causation is a problem, it is something that we will not be able to get away from in a no-fault system scheme. From cases in the common law such as *Wilsher v. Essex Health Authority*, we may conclude that plaintiffs have to prove that, on a balance of probabilities, a breach of duty of care caused the plaintiff's injury. Could it not be argued, as Lord Wilberforce did in *McGhee v. National Coal Board*, that in cases where neither the plaintiff nor the defendant could prove the precise causes of a disease and where the plaintiff had proved that the defendant had failed to observe a precaution designed to safeguard the plaintiff against a particular risk of injury and that injury materialised, it was for the defendant to prove that the injury did not result from his negligence? Would this reversal of the burden of proof help to get round the great difficulty in medicinal product liability cases, namely that of proving that the drug caused the injury, and would this overcome the difficulties of introducing no-fault compensation if it was included as part of such a regime?

**Mr Dodds-Smith**: I do not think it is justified to reverse the burden of proof on this central issue. We can always play about with it, but it then becomes a question of social engineering rather than legal reasoning. In the USA, if it cannot be proved which manufacturer's product was used, all manufacturers of that product will be liable according to their market share: it has nothing to do with the merits of the case, but is just concerned with distributing money. If the burden of proof in actions for negligence is reversed in certain circumstances and, in relation to strict liability, negligence is done away with in principle except for unknowable design defects, I think it is only reasonable that somebody wishing to make a claim about a product must carry the burden of showing that its use caused the injury. If the burden of proof on causation is also reversed, I believe that the concept might just as well be abandoned. It is not reasonable to ask a defendant to prove a negative here, but it is reasonable to expect a plaintiff to show, on the balance of probability, that a drug has caused an injury. People involved in these cases know their complexity, and I believe that showing causation will remain a major problem whatever system is adopted.

My concern is that the way in which the legal process deals with claims at the moment is heavily criticised, but the criticism should be directed not at deficiencies in the law but rather towards problems of access to justice, the problem of people not being able to afford to go to court, which is a major difficulty.

# 6 | Harmonisation of European controls over research: ethics committees, consent, compensation and indemnity

## Christopher Hodges[1]

*Partner, McKenna & Co, Solicitors, London*

---

## Background

The ethical justification for seeking to control medical research arises out of the need to balance a number of important but possibly conflicting principles. On the one hand, there is the aim of the advancement of knowledge, particularly scientific knowledge which would be of benefit to the health and safety of the community as a whole. On the other hand, there is the need to ensure personal human integrity and the individual's right to self-determination, which leads to concepts of informed consent and ensuring that the research subjects are exposed to minimum risk and inconvenience. The basic principles were set out in the Nuremberg Code 1949 and the Declaration of Helsinki 1964,[2] which may be summarised as giving rise to the following practical results:

— the subject should give voluntary consent;
— the research should produce fruitful results for the good of society which are unprocurable by any other means;
— the design of the study, prior animal work, existing knowledge and anticipated results justify the research;
— all unnecessary suffering and injury should be avoided.

Institutional Review Boards have been established on a statutory basis in the USA for some years.[3] Within Europe, there has been no systematic legal control over medical research. Such law as there has been on this topic has comprised limited and passing references within national legislation, which is essentially directed at controlling the availability of medicinal products rather than the conduct of medical research *per se*. Thus, Section 31 of the UK Medicines Act 1968 prohibits the sale or supply etc of any medicinal product for the purposes of a clinical trial except by the holder of a product licence or where a clinical trial certificate has been issued. The liberality of the regulatory regime in practice is illustrated by the existence of the clinical trial exemption (CTX) scheme[4] and the fact that Section 31 of the Act does not relate to products for research in healthy volunteers since such products are excluded from the definition of medicinal product in Section 130(4) of the Act. The sole reference to ethics committees in the Medicines Act appears in the Order relating to notification of clinical trial proposals and provides that any refusal by an ethics committee to approve a trial must be reported by the sponsor to the licensing authority. The German Drug Law of 1976 contains three sections[5] dealing specifically with protection of humans in clinical trials but does not refer to ethics committees or independent review of trial protocols.

The death of two volunteers in 1984, one in Ireland and one in Wales, acted as a spur to the introduction of national legislation in the Republic of Ireland and France. However, in both cases, legislation introduced in 1987 needed to be amended in 1990.[6] Clinical research is also dealt with in the Spanish Medicines Law of 1990.[7]

Although there has therefore been virtually no European regulation of clinical trials as such apart from these two statutes, there has for many years been a requirement that the results of clinical trials must be included in the application for a marketing authorisation for a product.[8] Thus, Part 3 of the Annex to Directive 75/318/EEC specifies that clinical trials must:

1. Always be preceded by adequate pharmacological and toxicological tests carried out on animals.
2. Be 'controlled' clinical trials.
3. As far as possible, and particularly in trials where the effect of the product cannot be objectively measured, be 'double blind'.
4. Be based on sufficiently precise criteria to permit a statistical analysis, if this is necessary. Inclusion of a large number of patients in a trial must not be regarded as an adequate substitute for a properly controlled trial.

In 1987, the Working Party of the Efficacy of Drugs of the Committee of Proprietary Medicinal Products (CPMP) published its *Recommended basis for the conduct of clinical trials of medicinal products in the European Community*.[9] The aims of this Report were tentative:

1. To define a general scientific framework, including basic methodology as well as ethical principles, for the conduct of clinical trials so

that optimal and relevant data are generated, and the results are recognised by the authorities of all Member States.

2. To describe the regulatory and administrative requirements of the Member States governing the conduct of clinical trials, in order to facilitate the task of a pharmaceutical company or others wishing to carry out multi-centre studies in more than one country.

3. To use the above-mentioned as a starting point for the efforts to establish a greater degree of convergence in the various regulatory and administrative requirements governing the conduct of clinical trials to be performed in the European Community. Thus, the results of such trials may eventually be enclosed as documentation in applications for marketing authorisation filed with the National Drug Regulatory Agencies of the Member States or with the CPMP.

The CPMP's Report noted that the systems of ethical review of protocols operated in most countries without relation to the approval systems applied by drug regulatory agencies. Accordingly, the Report stated that:

> No trial should be started before an independent review board or a similar institution dealing with research ethics has accepted the protocol. . . . the ethical evaluation should be made in accordance with the Declaration of Helsinki . . . . It is mandatory that all considerations about protection of human subjects are carried out in the spirit of the Declaration of Helsinki. . . . The voluntary informed and preferably written consent of the patient or the healthy volunteer to participation in a trial must be obtained.

The Report went on to list under 16 general headings information which should be included in research protocols. Despite the reference to considerations being 'mandatory', the CPMP's Report did not enjoy any legal status.

## Good Clinical Practice

In May 1990, the continued work of the CPMP's Working Party on Efficacy of Medicinal Products led to its adoption of *Good Clinical Practice for trials on medicinal products in the European Community*. The document was referred to as a guideline, with the stated objective 'to establish the principles of the standard of Good Clinical Practice for trials on medicinal products in human beings with the EEC'. The good clinical practice (GCP) guidelines begin with the following summary, and the principles are to apply to all four phases of research:

> All parties involved in the evaluation of medicinal products share the responsibility of accepting and working according to such standards in mutual trust and confidence. Pre-established, systematic written procedures for the organisation, conduct, data collection, documentation and verification of clinical trials are necessary to ensure that the rights

and integrity of the trial subjects are fairly protected and to establish the credibility of data and to improve the ethical, scientific and technical quality of trials. These procedures also include good statistical design as an essential prerequisite for credibility of data and moreover, it is unethical to enlist the co-operation of human subjects in trials which are not adequately designed. By these means all data, information and documents may be confirmed as being properly generated, recorded and reported.

The GCP guidelines extend the principle of protection of subjects into detailed control over not only the design of clinical trials but also their conduct. Not only must the protocol be reviewed to confirm that the research is ethical and will yield reliable data of the best quality, but also all activities which are to be carried out during the research must be undertaken on the same basis. Accordingly, the guidelines include detailed chapters on data handling, statistics and quality assurance.

## Comments on the European guidelines

### Legal basis

The European Commission moved quickly in mid-1990 to propose that the CPMP's Guidelines should have the force of law. The method which has been adopted is a proposal to amend the Annex to Directive 75/318/EEC[10] by adapting these existing requirements to technical progress. The advantage of this procedure is that the Commission's proposal is considered by a Standing Committee of representatives of Member States, which acts by qualified majority. The Commission then adopts the proposal within three months. GCP could therefore be adopted as community law extremely quickly. The initial draft proposal was very brief and stated as follows:

1.1 All phases of clinical investigation, including bio-availability and bio-equivalent studies, shall be designed, implemented and reported in accordance with Good Clinical Practice.

1.2 All clinical trials shall be carried out in accordance with the ethical principles laid down in the Declaration of Helsinki. The freely given informed consent of each trial subject shall be obtained and documented. The trial protocol, procedures and documentation shall be submitted by the sponsor and/or investigator for an opinion to an ethics committee. The trials shall not begin before the opinion of this committee has been received in writing.

1.3 Pre-established, systematic written procedures for the organisation, conduct, data collection, documentation and verification of clinical trials shall be required. These procedures shall also include good statistical design as an essential prerequisite for credibility of data.

It will be seen that the provision in Paragraph 1.2 that informed consent is required from each trial subject does not cover the situation where the subject is incapable of giving consent, such as where he or she is unconscious, a child or under mental disability. The relevant passages in the GCP guidelines themselves on this point are discussed further below.

One preliminary comment can be made on the language used in the guidelines. In common with much European Community (EC) legislation, the Report is written in a clear, straightforward style. This approach has the benefit of brevity but, to an English lawyer at least, raises a succession of questions on the construction of the precise words used which could give rise to ambiguities or issues as to whether particular situations are or are not covered or as to precise procedural formalities. As with European legislation, when GCP is implemented within the Community, one would expect these points to be clarified in national legislation, but possibly at a cost of increased complexity and lack of consistency from state to state.

Having made this proposal for legislation on GCP, the Commission had further thoughts and produced a discussion paper in February 1991 on whether there was a need for a new Directive dealing specifically with GCP. Although amending the Directive on testing (75/318) would harmonise and achieve many of the objectives set out in the CPMP guidelines, there would remain matters such as

— inspection of trials and sites;
— an investigative new drug (IND) approach to obligatory notification of clinical trials to regulatory authorities and manufacturing authorisation/Good Manufacturing Practice (GMP) for investigational products and labelling;
— establishment of a confidential community database of clinical trial notifications, open only to regulatory authorities.

The Commission discussion paper states that a legislative underpinning of GCP standards is essential in order for EC clinical trials to be acceptable to non-EC authorities and to assist in the prevention of fraud. Any Directive on GCP will, of course, need to be enacted in the domestic legislation or administrative action of each member state, and this will inevitably continue differences between states, as can be seen from the existing French and Irish legislation (discussed below).

*GCP framework of ethics committees*

The GCP guidelines define an ethics committee as:

> an independent body, constituted by medical professionals and non-medical members, whose responsibility is to verify that the safety,

integrity and human rights of the subjects participating in a particular trial are protected, thereby providing public reassurance.

Ethics committees should be constituted and operated so that the suitability of the investigators, facilities, protocols, the eligibility of trial subject groups, and the adequacy of confidentiality safeguards may be objectively and impartially reviewed independently of the investigator, sponsor, and relevant authorities.

The legal status, constitution, and regulatory requirements pertaining to ethics committees, review boards or similar institutions may differ among countries.

A list of the members of the ethics committee and their positions, and a description of its working procedures, including response times, should be publicly available.

Chapter 1 of the guidelines expands on the role of ethics committees in the protection of trial subjects. After stating that the Declaration of Helsinki is the accepted basis for clinical trial ethics, it is said that:

> 1.2   The personal integrity and welfare of the trial subjects is the ultimate responsibility of the *investigator* in relation to the trial; but independent assurance that subjects are protected is provided by an ethics committee and freely obtained informed consent. (*emphasis added*)

It can therefore be seen that the granting of an approval to a trial by an ethics committee in no way alters or displaces the responsibilities and obligations of the sponsor, monitor and investigators concerned in the trial. The role of an ethics committee is one of independent verification in order to provide public reassurance. The emphasis is stated to be on *public* reassurance rather than reassurance to individual subjects who may take part in the trial. This may be of relevance in considering whether members of ethics committees owe research subjects any duty of care (see below). It also becomes clear on consideration of the more detailed provisions of the European guidelines that the ethics committees are intended to assume a role, which in practice has been pushed rather beyond the bounds of review of the ethical validity of the research from a strict scientific standpoint to include functions which could be characterised as essentially of a regulatory nature. The guidelines, therefore, constitute devolution of regulatory powers to ethics committees in place of centralised licensing authorities. It could be said that the power of self-regulation is being devolved to scientists in a more informal context rather than being held centrally by administrators in a more bureaucratic context. Examples of the expanding regulatory function of ethics committees include the requirement to be informed of all subsequent protocol amendments and of serious or unexpected adverse events occurring during the trial,[11] and the obligation to consider:

> the suitability of the investigator for the proposed trial in relation to his/her qualifications, experience, supporting staff, and available facilities, on the basis of the information available to the committee.[12]

Although the GCP guidelines do not state this specifically, recent reports of the Royal College of Physicians (RCP) recommend that ethics committees should not only require annual progress reports from investigators and copies of any published reports but, consistent with the requirement to consider the suitability of the investigator, staff and facilities, also interview investigators in person and carry out site visits where appropriate.[13] It will be interesting to see to what extent ethics committees fulfil regulatory/monitoring roles in practice.

It is relevant to contrast the approach taken in the recent French, Irish and Spanish legislation on clinical research,[14] which all provide that permission to carry out research is under the control of the Minister of Health but that the opinion of an ethical committee must first be obtained. The French legislation is supplemented by detailed decrees and a fixed regional network of ethics committees. Under none of these systems is there a requirement for continued monitoring by the committees or for adverse reactions to be reported to them: their role appears to cease after initial approval has been given (subject to possible reconsideration of amendments to the protocol) and regulatory responsibility passes to the regulatory authorities.

A particular problem currently arises in practice over multi-centre trials. The European GCP guidelines have not grasped the nettle of specifying that a protocol need be submitted to only one (perhaps central) ethics committee rather than to all committees in whose district the trial will be carried out. This would greatly simplify the administrative burden and save time for company sponsors, who are sometimes faced with widely varying requirements from different committees for the same protocol.

## Matters for consideration by an ethics committee

The GCP guidelines state that an ethics committee should be asked to 'consider' matters under six given headings. This wording gives rise to some ambiguity as to the extent to which the listed matters are exclusive and mandatory. The matters are:

(a) The suitability of the investigator . . . supporting staff and available facilities . . .
(b) The suitability of the protocol in relation to the objectives of the

study, its scientific efficiency, i.e. a potential for reaching sound conclusions with the smallest possible exposure of subjects, and the justification of predictable risks and inconveniences weighed against the anticipated benefits of the subjects and/or others.

(c) The adequacy and completeness of the written information to be given to the subjects, their relatives, guardians and, if necessary, legal representatives.

(d) The means by which initial recruitment is to be conducted and by which full information is to be given, and by which consent is to be obtained. All written information for the subject and/or legal representative must be submitted in its final form.

(e) Provision for compensation/treatment in the case of injury or death of a subject if attributable to a clinical trial, and any insurance or indemnity to cover the liability of the investigator and sponsor.

(f) The extent to which investigators and subjects may be rewarded/compensated for participation.

The particular issues of consent and compensation are considered below in more detail.

## National development of ethics committees

In the UK, ethics committees are not currently established or regulated by statute. Their history can be traced through reports of the Medical Research Council and RCP in 1973 and a Department of Health and Social Security (DHSS) Circular of 1975.[15] The Department of Health (DoH) issued a draft Health Circular in October 1989, which remained in draft until 1991, no doubt in view of the European developments relating to GCP. The final DoH Guidelines[15a] specify that all Health Authorities should establish Local Research Ethics Committees (LRECs) by 1 February 1992 to which all protocols which involve personnel or facilities of the Health Authority should be submitted. The LRECs should have 8–12 members 'of sound judgement and relevant experience', including hospital medical staff, nursing staff, general practitioners (GPs) and two or more lay persons.

In contrast, a decree[16] under the French law specifies that each regional advisory committee shall consist of 12 permanent members, each of which is to have a specific specialisation. There are to be four researchers, one GP, two pharmacists, and one each of a nurse, a person qualified in ethical matters, a person active in the social field, a psychologist and a lawyer. Each member shall also have an alternate. At least six members must be present for a valid decision to be made, four of whom must be from particular categories of specialisation. Members are chosen at random from a list of candidates drawn up by the regional government on nominations from relevant bodies. The members receive no remuneration but their expenses are defrayed. The

French law also specifies that all places where healthy volunteer research is to be carried out must be authorised by the regional government.

The French legislation is therefore extremely detailed. This is not the case with the Irish legislation, since there is little call for permanent ethics committees to be established there on a regional basis. For each individual trial, the membership of a proposed committee has to be submitted to the minister, who will approve it if he considers that

> the committee ... is competent to consider the justification for conducting the proposed clinical trial and the circumstances under which it is to be conducted.[17]

The composition of the committee may at any time be changed with the approval of the minister.[18] Non-statutory guidelines encourage the selection of committees to include lay, legal and business representation as well as medical and paramedical expertise.

The Spanish law is a little more detailed, specifying that ethics committees

> should be constituted, at least, by an interdisciplinary team made up of medical doctors, hospital pharmacists, clinical pharmacologists, nursing personnel and persons unrelated with health professionals of which, at least one, shall be a jurist.[19]

The UK DoH Guidelines make clear that the decision whether to approve the proposed research rests with the health authority, and that the LREC's function is limited to advice and does not include the power to decide. The Guidelines say that 'standing orders should be determined by the DHA'.[20] The approach is therefore similar to that of the Medicines Act 1968, under which regulatory power rests with the licensing authority and the Section 4 committees are merely advisory— at least in theory.

Similarly, the French, Irish and Spanish legislation provides that the ultimate decision on an application rests with the minister.[21] Curiously, neither the French nor Irish legislation specifies any criteria on which the minister may exercise his power—there is not even a reference to the Declaration of Helsinki. This is in contrast to the extensive criteria specified in that legislation for consideration by an ethics committee. The Spanish law, however, does specify that clinical trials must:

— only be undertaken after sufficient scientific data are available which guarantees that the risks are reasonable;
— be conducted in accordance with the Declaration of Helsinki;
— only be commenced if there is reasonable doubt as to the efficacy and safety of the matter to be tested.[22]

As far as procedure is concerned, positive ministerial approval is required in Ireland, within 12 weeks of the application and after consultation with the National Drugs Advisory Board. In France, there is a negative approval system on a similar basis to the UK CTX system: the sponsor forwards a letter of intent to the minister together with the opinion of the committee. Spain requires positive authorisation by the Ministry of Health and Consumption, but the law also establishes a negative approval system under which the ministry has 60 days to object in the case of further similar trials of a product for which one clinical trial has already been approved, and of trials for new dosages or indications of medicines already licensed.[23]

## Informed consent

Paragraph 1.2 of the CPMP guidelines states that independent assurance that subjects are protected is provided not only by an ethics committee but also by 'freely obtained informed consent'. Informed consent is defined in the CPMP guidelines as:

> The voluntary confirmation of a subject's willingness to participate in a particular trial, and the documentation thereof. This confirmation should only be sought after information has been given about the trial including an explanation of its objectives, potential benefits and risks and inconveniences, and of the subject's rights and responsibilities in accordance with the current revision of the Declaration of Helsinki.

The guidelines make no exception for giving research subjects the appropriate information and obtaining their consent, other than in the case of incapacity (discussed below). The guidelines do not specify the extent of the disclosure required in terms of the detail of possible risks. In North America, the 'doctrine of informed consent' requires that full information needs to be given, as judged by the patient: the English common law approach is that in order to establish a defence to a claim for trespass to the person, the consent must be real in that the volunteer must be informed in broad terms of the nature and general purpose of the study and the consent must not be procured by fraud or misrepresentation.[24] In relation to advice on risks, the English rule under negligence principles is that there is no difference between the standard of care required in giving advice on risks and that required in diagnosis and treatment. The primary obligation to disclose risks with a view to allowing the patient to make a rational choice has been re-emphasised, but the obligation has been limited to making such disclosure as is reasonable in the light of all the circumstances, so that the physician will normally have discharged his duty if he acts in accordance with practice accepted as proper by a body of physicians skilled in the relevant field.[25] The extent of disclosure in any given case is therefore judged not by the patient but by the doctor.

The guidelines contain a number of paragraphs which outline the following procedure for obtaining informed consent:[26]

— information should be given in both oral and written form whenever possible;
— subjects, their relatives, guardians or, if necessary, legal representatives, must be given ample opportunity to enquire about details of the trial. This provision is confusingly drafted. If legal consent is required only from the research subject and he or she is capable of giving such consent, is it a requirement that relatives should be given information about the trial and an opportunity to enquire and, if so, how many relatives? It was presumably intended that the opportunity to enquire is only relevant to the person or persons whose consent is legally required in any given case, or to the parents or legal representatives where the subject is a child or under some mental incapacity, where it is good practice (even though it may not be a strict legal requirement) to obtain their consent;
— subjects must be allowed sufficient time to decide whether or not they wish to participate. This time, the guidelines do not specifically refer to parents, guardians etc although the same provision ought to apply to them;
— the subject must have access to information about the procedures for compensation and treatment. The guidelines do not state that such information must be accessible before giving consent. This is presumably a deliberate omission since there are certain situations in which reference to compensation for injury might alarm patients about to undergo particular procedures. On the other hand, it might be said that the guidelines could be clearer in specifying who is to provide such information and in what manner.

Once consent has been obtained, it must be recorded. Paragraph 1.12 of the guidelines states that:

> Consent must be documented either by the subject's dated signature or by the signature of an independent witness who records the subject's assent. In either case the signature confirms that the consent is based on information which has been understood, and that the subject has freely chosen to participate without prejudice to legal and ethical rights while allowing the possibility of withdrawal from the study without having to give any reason unless adverse events have occurred.

If the subject is incapable of giving consent he may be included, provided that the ethics committee has agreed in principle and if the investigator is of the opinion that participation will promote the welfare and interest of the subject. The agreement of a legally valid representative that participation will promote the welfare and interest of the subject should also be recorded by a dated signature. If neither signed informed consent nor witnessed signed verbal consent is possible, this fact must be documented, with reasons, by the investigator.

In the case of a non-therapeutic study, the guidelines say that consent must always be given by the signature of the subject personally.[27] This accords with practice, in that a signature will, of course, normally be obtained on the contractual consent form between the healthy volunteer and sponsor. This provision is, however, likely to inhibit further Phase I research in young children and people suffering from some mental incapacity. This is an area in which it is particularly difficult to reconcile the competing principles of the advancement of knowledge and the protection of an individual's right to self-determination (which, in the case of persons with limited or no mental capacity, is usually taken to mean their best interests).

The only exception allowable to informed consent under the guidelines is where the volunteer is incapable of giving consent. Some doctors, such as cancer researchers or cardiologists, argue that GCP guidelines should provide for circumstances in which it would not be in the interests of the research and/or of certain patients that adequate information on risks should be given or even that sometimes they should be told they are involved in research. This is another area in which it is certainly difficult to reconcile the competing principles, and the CPMP has again come down on the side of individuals' rights.

Another provision which is likely to raise legal difficulties is Paragraph 1.15 which states:

> Any information becoming available during the trial which may be of relevance for the trial subjects must be made known to them by the investigator.

This, once more, is entirely consistent with the principle that an individual has a right to self-determination. The approach taken is that this right does not cease merely because a healthy or patient volunteer agrees to take part in a research project. However, some doctors might criticise this approach. The practical legal difficulty arises in determining whether any information has become available during the trial which may have some implications for safety. Information in a randomised double-blind clinical trial which has been recorded but not unblinded would presumably not satisfy the test, but it is quite possible that other information will come to the attention of investigators or monitors. The information might be fairly limited in scope and difficult to interpret: should it in fact be passed on to all trial subjects, some or all of whom might be unduly disturbed to hear it?

## Compensation

It is important to remember that research subjects are unlikely to be able successfully to claim compensation for injury at law. Severe difficulties exist in establishing negligence or strict liability in the research context. In the former case, there is the test of reasonableness and the defence of *volenti non fit injuria* (in English law), and in strict liability there is the need to establish that the product was defective and to overcome the 'state of the art' defence. In both cases, there is also the burden of establishing causation, although some Member States have reversed the burden of proof. These hurdles therefore need to be overcome by other means. In Sweden, Finland and New Zealand, of course, the law is different and compensation is paid on a no-fault basis, provided that there is some basic evidence of causation, to supplement the social security regime. In Germany, drug manufacturers are subject to an insurance based compensation system with absolute liability.[28]

By paragraph 2.3(j) of the GCP guidelines, the sponsor has the following responsibilities:

> To provide adequate compensation/treatment for subjects in the event of trial related injury or death, and provide indemnity (legal and financial cover) for the investigator, except for claims resulting from malpractice and/or negligence.

Paragraph 9 of the Annex to the guidelines states that subjects must be 'satisfactorily insured', although the meaning of the word 'insured' is unclear in this context. A number of questions arise with this wording:

— who is to compensate an injured subject where the injury arises wholly or partly as a result of negligence by the investigator? Is the sponsor solely responsible (presumably with the right of a claim against a negligent investigator)? Do the words 'except for claims resulting from malpractice and/or negligence' qualify the manufacturer's obligation to compensate the subject or qualify the manufacturer's obligation to indemnify the investigator, or both? The list of responsibilities of an investigator at Paragraph 2.5 does not include any obligation to compensate in the event of negligence or to hold insurance;

— is the subject covered for injury sustained as a result of *participation* in a trial, as well as where the injury is directly caused by the trial product? Such injuries would include those caused by placebo or drugs used as a comparison or control, or procedures involved in the trial;

— how much is 'adequate' compensation? Is this to be left to the
  differing national implementing legislation or would consistency be
  beneficial?
— this provision would apply in the case of post-marketing studies
  since the guidelines expressly cover Phase IV trials. This has not
  previously been the general position in the UK, since compensation
  for injury caused by licensed medicinal products is based on the
  existing law of product liability and negligence, although the Association of the British Pharmaceutical Industry's (ABPI's) 1991
  revised compensation guidelines have been extended to cover
  injury caused by procedures under the protocol rather than the
  drug under trial.

Under the GCP guidelines, provisions for compensation, insurance
and indemnity are matters which must be reviewed by the ethics
committee.[29] This, again, extends current law and practice. Ethics
committees in the UK are expected to consider compensation arrangements but are not currently expected to consider insurance or indemnity provisions. Indeed, the view of the RCP is that indemnities are
not the proper concern of ethics committees, 'but rather should be left
to the parties to negotiate as they see fit'.[30]

The UK DoH Guidelines specify very little on the subject of compensation. The primary obligation is merely that:

> The LREC should ensure that those who agree to participate in research
> which may involve some risk, whether as patients or healthy volunteers,
> are told at the outset what arrangements will apply in their case.[31]

The UK Guidelines go on to note that National Health Service (NHS)
bodies are not empowered to offer advance indemnity to participants,
who are left legally to pursue a claim for negligence through litigation.
A reference to the fact that such participants may be offered a without
prejudice *ex gratia* payment was deleted from the final version of the
Guidelines.[20] This situation was criticised by the RCP Report (as
referred to below).

In the case of private sector companies, the UK Guidelines note that:

> LRECs would seek confirmation that any such company conducting or
> sponsoring a patient or healthy volunteer study *accepts responsibility* for
> compensation and provides details of the *basis* on which it will be
> provided i.e. causation, fault etc. plus *evidence of their ability to fulfil it*.
> (*emphasis added*).

This approach is markedly more lax than the legislation in France
and Ireland—and even the 1976 German legislation. There is, surprisingly, no requirement that compensation should be paid without
the need to prove fault and there is no mention of the ABPI guidelines

or of the GCP's reference to insurance cover. The wording in fact
follows that of the Medicines Commission's 1982 *Advice to health
ministers on healthy volunteer studies* but with a relaxation from that
Advice in relation to 'no-fault' compensation:

> All companies conducting healthy volunteer studies should be expected
> to accept responsibility for 'no-fault' compensation and provide evi-
> dence of their ability to fulfil it.

The phrase 'evidence of their ability to fulfil [payment of compensa-
tion]' is imprecise and gives LRECs little practical guidance. How
much evidence is required: a copy of the latest audited accounts or of
the current bank statement? Is such a financial and accounting enquiry
properly the function of an ethics committee or in fact a function which
should be undertaken by a regulatory official? In contrast, the RCP
took the view in 1990:

> If a proper undertaking to compensate in accordance with applicable
> guidelines is given by an established company it is probably not appro-
> priate for an ethics committee to enquire whether it will be discharged
> out of company funds or the proceeds of an insurance policy — these are
> matters for the company to decide[32]

The German Drug Law specifies that insurance must be held which
must stand in appropriate relation to the risks involved in the clinical
trial and in the case of death or permanent disability must total at least
DM 500,000.[33]

The recent legislation in Ireland, France and Spain also provides for
consideration of insurance. Under a French decree a sponsor has to
hold quite a high level of insurance: cover of at least FFr 5 million per
victim, FFr 30 million per research protocol and FFr 50 million for all
claims made in an insurance year must be held until 10 years after the
end of the research.[34] The Irish Act is silent on the question of the basis
of compensation. It provides merely that the sponsor and investigator
must establish to the satisfaction of the minister in advance of each trial
on a case by case basis that they have sufficient security to provide for
payments of damages on their own behalf if they are personally
negligent.[35] This does not give rise to an obligation to pay compensation as such, on any basis. 'Security' is defined as including a contract of
insurance, a contract of indemnity, a guarantee, a surety, a warranty
and a bond.[36] Neither the Spanish law nor the Irish legislation and
guidelines mention any financial sums or limits. However the Spanish
law does include some interesting provisions.[37] First, a trial can only be
started if 'insurance covering the damages' is in place. This presumably
refers to damages which might be awarded by a Spanish court, but up
to what level? Compensation for many injuries might be awarded at a

trivial level, but equally it might be the case that very high damages might be awarded in individual cases. Although regulations might be made under the Spanish law which set further guidelines, the approach seems to be to leave the risk with the promoter, chief researcher and owner of the hospital or centre in question, since the law specifically provides that these people shall be severally liable without proof of fault if the insurance does not cover the damages. It is, of course, inherent in this approach that the appropriate level of damages should be set by a court: there is no specific arbitration or mediation procedure under the law, unlike the approach under the UK ABPI guidelines. The Spanish law does, however, assist the injured research subject by reversing the burden of proof in his favour for injuries which occur during the trial or within one year after its termination.

Recurrent questions arise in relation to compensation for injury as to who should bear the responsibility for compensation in the event of the subject suffering injury which might not be attributable to the compound under research. The French statute and the various ABPI guidelines attempt to deal with this point, but are perhaps not entirely successful.

The provisions of the French law relating to compensation essentially place the responsibility for compensation on the sponsor, whether in non-therapeutic or therapeutic research, irrespective of the negligence of the investigator, although the wording in the latter case is ambiguous:

> In case of biomedical research with no direct benefit to the individual, the sponsor, even when not at fault, takes responsibility for the compensation of any harmful effects of the research on a person undergoing it, notwithstanding the possible action of a third party or the voluntary withdrawal of the person who initially consented to undergo the research.

> In case of biomedical research with direct benefit to the individual, the sponsor takes responsibility for the compensation of any harmful effects of the research on a person undergoing it, unless he proves that such adverse effects are not attributable to his or any participating party's action, notwithstanding the possible action of a third party or the voluntary withdrawal of the person who initially consented to undergo the research.

> In all biomedical research, the sponsor shall take out insurance covering his and any other participating party's liability as it results from this article, irrespective of the relationship between the sponsor and the participating parties. The provisions of this article are binding on all parties.[38]

The essential burden for compensation is therefore firmly on the sponsor. In the case of research in healthy volunteers, the burden is absolute and negligence of an investigator is, at least as between sponsor and subject, irrelevant. However, the provisions of the second paragraph, dealing with research in patients, are somewhat ambiguous as to the extent to which proof of the action of a third party excuses the sponsor.

In the UK the provision of compensation for research injury is left to a non-statutory regime, dependent merely upon whether or not the sponsor and/or contract research house in fact abide by the ABPI guidelines. Curiously, the DoH Guidelines are entirely silent on the advisability of or any requirement for adherence to the ABPI guidelines. Different ABPI guidelines cover different types of research:

## Non-patient human volunteers: 1988 ABPI guidelines

The relationship between the volunteer and the sponsor should be governed by the terms of a written contract included in the consent form which the volunteer signs to signify his agreement to take part in the study. The ABPI guidelines state:

11.7 The agreement should clearly record the obligation the pharmaceutical company or research establishment has accepted in terms of financial rewards for participation and compensation in the event of injury. In particular, the volunteer should be given a clear commitment that in the event of bodily injury he will receive appropriate compensation without having to prove either that such injury arose through negligence or that the product was defective in the sense that it did not fulfil a reasonable expectation of safety. The agreement should not seek to remove that right of the volunteer, as an alternative, to pursue a claim on the basis of either negligence or strict liability if he is so minded.

11.8 Where pharmaceutical companies sponsor studies to be performed in outside research establishments, the responsibility for paying compensation should be clarified and reflected in the contractual documentation with the volunteer. Where the sponsor company is to provide the undertaking regarding compensation, it is recommended that the sponsor company enters into an unqualified obligation to pay compensation to the volunteer on proof of causation, having previously protected its rights to recourse against the research establishment in its agreement with that establishment, to cover the position where the negligence of its contractor may have caused or contributed to the injury by the volunteer. A volunteer can reasonably expect that compensation will be paid quickly and that any dispute regarding who will finally bear the cost of the compensation paid to him will be resolved separately by the other parties to the research.

A model agreement is attached to the guidelines, in which the relevant clauses read:

8(iii)  In the event of my suffering any significant deterioration in health or well-being caused directly by my participation in the study, compensation will be paid to me by the company.

(iv)  The amount of such compensation shall be calculated by reference to the amount of damages commonly awarded for similar injuries by an English court if liability is admitted, provided that such compensation may be reduced to the extent that I, by reason of contributory fault, am partly responsible for the injury (or where I have received equivalent payment for such injury under any policy of insurance effected by the company for my benefit);

Negligence by an investigator is therefore irrelevant as far as a claim by an injured party for compensation is concerned. He is to be paid forthwith by the sponsor, who may then have a claim against the investigator (and the contractual documentation between them should provide for this). There is also a provision for arbitration in the event of a dispute over payment of compensation.

In 1986, the RCP criticised the fact that compensation for injury suffered as a result of research conducted in and sponsored by universities, NHS hospitals, the Medical Research Council and other similar establishments is not covered by any guideline commitment but is dependent on an *ex gratia* payment.[39]

We believe that universities and other institutions should make binding commitments to provide compensation, because we consider it unacceptable that a healthy volunteer should have to rely on an *ex gratia* payment.

## Patient volunteers: 1991 ABPI guidelines

The 1983 guidelines were revised in 1991 in the light of developing considerations, especially the 1990 Report of the RCP's Working Party, *Research involving patients*. The relationship between the sponsor and subject is, in the case of Phases II and III research, not contractual and the guidelines state that the sponsor's assurance to abide by them is 'without legal commitment'.

1.2  Compensation should be paid when, on the balance of probabilities, the injury was attributable to the administration of a medicinal product under trial or any clinical intervention or procedure provided for by the protocol that would not have occurred but for the inclusion of the patient in the trial.

1.3  Compensation should be paid to a child injured *in utero* through the participation of the subject's mother in a clinical trial as if the child were a patient-volunteer with the full benefit of these guidelines.

1.4 Compensation should only be paid for the more serious injury of an enduring and disabling character (including exacerbation of an existing condition) and not for temporary pain or discomfort or less serious or curable complaints.

1.5 Where there is an adverse reaction to a medicinal product under trial and injury is caused by a procedure adopted to deal with that adverse reaction, compensation should be paid for such injury as if it were caused directly by the medicinal product under trial.

1.6 Neither the fact that the adverse reaction causing the injury was foreseeable or predictable, nor the fact that the patient has freely consented (whether in writing or otherwise) to participate in the trial should exclude a patient from consideration for compensation under these guidelines, although compensation may be abated or excluded in the light of the factors described in paragraph 4.2 below.

1.7 For the avoidance of doubt, compensation should be paid regardless of whether the patient is able to prove that the company has been negligent in relation to research or development of the medicinal product under trial or that the product is defective and therefore, as the producer, the company is subject to strict liability in respect of injuries caused by it.

. . . . .

4.1 The amount of compensation paid should be appropriate to the nature, severity and persistence of the injury and should in general terms be consistent with the quantum of damages commonly awarded for similar injuries by an English court in cases where legal liability is admitted.

4.2 Compensation may be abated, or in certain circumstances excluded, in the light of the following factors (on which will depend the level of risk the patient can reasonably be expected to accept):

4.2.1 the seriousness of the disease being treated, the degree of probability that adverse reactions will occur and any warnings given;

4.2.2 the risks and benefits of established treatments relative to those known or suspected of the trial medicine.

This reflects the fact that flexibility is required given the particular patient's circumstances. As an extreme example, there may be a patient suffering from a serious or life-threatening disease who is warned of a certain defined risk of adverse reaction. Participation in the trial is then based on an expectation that the benefit/risk ratio associated with participation may be better than that associated with alternative treatment. It is, therefore, reasonable that the patient accepts the high risk and should not expect compensation for the occurrence of the adverse reaction of which he or she was told.

There is provision for arbitration by an independent expert in the event of any difference of opinion.

Compensation is excluded, however, where

1. The product failed to have its intended effect.
2. The injury was caused by another licensed medicinal product which was administered as a comparison with the product under trial.
3. A placebo has failed to provide a therapeutic benefit.

Compensation should not be paid, or should be abated, to the extent that the injury has arisen through:

1. A significant departure from the agreed protocol.
2. The wrongful act or default of a third party, including a doctor's failure to deal adequately with an adverse reaction.
3. Contributory negligence by the patient.

None of these exclusions represents a departure from the 1983 guidelines, except perhaps for the first, that 'the product failed to have its intended effect', which may have been implicit before.

The approach set out in these guidelines is a logical application of legal principles. The subject is given the considerable benefit of not having to prove negligence, but the guidelines do not constitute a 'no-fault' compensation scheme because of the applicability of rules on causation, most notably in the exclusions. The subject is also at a disadvantage because there is no legal commitment to pay by the sponsor. The RCP criticised the 1983 guidelines for this reason, and recommended that there should be a contractual commitment to compensate patient volunteers, perhaps with the investigator acting as the company's agent for this limited purpose.[40] The ABPI did not adopt this view in its 1991 revision. The matter is certainly not susceptible to a simple answer, since the imposition of a contractual relationship on a treatment situation which is not normally contractual is not a simple matter, either for reasons of achieving universality or practicability, or from the point of view of effecting an alteration in the nature of the patient–doctor relationship, with the potential for conflict that exists here. The ABPI would point to the absence of any practical problem over compensation which needs to be resolved: research injuries are fortunately extremely rare and companies are generally well aware of the need to avoid adverse criticism. In practice, the guidelines might therefore be interpreted liberally in any given case.

It is interesting to note that although the RCP recommended that compensation should be paid for *involvement* in research and not confined to injury due to a treatment under test itself (which the ABPI has adopted) and also to injury due to withholding active treatment (which the ABPI has not adopted), it did *not* recommend that compensation should be paid for injury due to a standard medicine used for comparison or to failure of a treatment to have its hoped for or intended effect. A strong case could, however, be made that these exclusions and the exclusion of placebo-induced injury should all be compensated. Again, it is possible that in practice a company might be well advised to avoid any unduly restrictive stance.

In its report of 1990, the RCP criticised the fact that patients injured in publicly funded research have to rely on an *ex gratia* and *ad hoc* system:

> ... patients ... [should be] compensated on an agreed basis which should be made clear to them before they consent . . . The absence of [a policy to compensate] should be treated as a material fact to be disclosed by the investigator to the patient.[41]

### Phase IV

The 1991 guidelines apply to Phase II and III trials and not to injury arising from clinical trials on marketed products where a product licence exists,

> except to the extent that the injury is caused to a patient as a direct result of *procedures undertaken* in accordance with the protocol (but not any product administered) to which the patient would not have been exposed had treatment been other than in the course of the trial.

*Guidelines on post-marketing surveillance 1988* are issued by the Joint Committee of the ABPI, the British Medical Association (BMA), the Committee on Safety of Medicines and the Royal College of General Practitioners (RCGP) and a *Code of practice for the clinical assessment of licensed medicinal products in general practice 1983* by joint agreement between the BMA, the RCGP and the ABPI. These do not, however, deal with compensation issues, which must be resolved under the general law.

### Volunteers

In the conduct of a sponsoring company's attitude towards payment of compensation, it should be remembered that participation in a trial is generally considered by insurers to be a material fact to be disclosed when a healthy volunteer makes a proposal for any health-related insurance or renews it. In its Advice to Health Ministers in 1987 (Paragraph 6.9) the Medicines Commission recommended that every healthy volunteer should be informed of this fact, and the model information document annexed to the ABPI 1988 guidelines includes this information.

## Indemnities to investigators or institutions

Investigators have long expected an indemnity in respect of claims not arising through their negligence. Investigators and institutions in which research takes place are now seeking more detailed information and support from sponsors. The RCP considered that such matters are not the proper concern of ethics committees:

> Such indemnities relate to protecting them rather than to protecting research subjects in the event that a claim arises. We do not consider that such indemnities are the proper concern of ethics committees, but rather should be left to the parties to negotiate as they see fit. These indemnities often provide for the handling of any legal proceedings by the company. This would not seem to disadvantage research subjects.[42]

This approach is not adopted in the GCP guidelines:

> Sponsor to provide . . . indemnity (legal and financial cover) for the investigator, except for claims resulting from malpractice and/or negligence.[43]

In this context, it should be remembered that these guidelines are expressed to cover Phase IV research as well.

Standard provisions which are often included in such contracts provide an indemnity for the investigator and his assistants for claims provided that the investigator has not been negligent, there has been no material failure to adhere to their protocol and the investigator notifies claims to the sponsor. As in virtually all insurance contracts, the company is given the right to take over conduct of the defence of any claim. The question of a parent company guarantee is sometimes raised, particularly if the sponsoring company is a local subsidiary with small capital and the trial or its effects may continue for some time.

## Insurance

It has been said above that insurance is compulsory for clinical research in France, Spain and Germany, although not elsewhere. The standard product liability policies available to manufacturers respond only in the case of a legal liability to pay; in other words, on proof of negligence or strict liability or under other legal rules. Such policies will not respond if the sponsor enters into a special contractual undertaking to pay on proof of causation, as is the scheme under the ABPI guidelines, unless the insurer has specifically agreed to this. Similarly, such policies will not respond to *ex gratia* payments other than by concession.

Insurance policies designed specifically for clinical trials have begun to be written in the past few years, so as to avoid the risk being borne solely by the company. However, these are usually written on a 'claims made' basis, and therefore need to be renewed each year. The premiums can also be high, for example, of the order of between £15 and £50 per patient for £1m cover. It is, of course, likely that such costs will fall as the market develops and if the incidence of claims continues to be very low.

The wording of policies needs to be carefully considered to ensure that the extent of cover and claims procedures will adequately cover the perceived risk. One standard policy, for example, sets out a detailed procedure for dealing with a claim by an injured subject, involving an offer to the subject which must be agreed by him within three months, and if this procedure is not followed, the policy will not respond.

## Legal responsibility of ethics committees

What effect will the establishment of ethics committees on a statutory basis have in the context of a research subject who suffers injury? What would be the position of an injured subject where there may have been negligence over design of the protocol, or a protocol which sanctions giving less than full information on certain risks to subjects or dispensing with some element of obtaining consent? Without going into great detail for present purposes, a general conclusion might be justified that such a claim against a sponsor or investigator would at least be weakened as a result of approval by an ethics committee, and in some cases might be extinguished. Issues of contribution by joint tortfeasors* might arise.

It is an open question whether members of an ethics committee which consented to a study could be sued in negligence by a research subject. An amendment to the Irish Act[44] specifically excludes such an action. However, it can be argued that there is no reason in principle why the general law of countries which have not made a statutory exclusion of liability should not hold that ethics committees, whose function is essentially to protect the rights of individual research subjects, should not owe such volunteers a duty of care. Reference could also be made to the fact that part of the function of ethics committees is to consider such matters as whether the research is of a sufficient standard of scientific design and conduct,[45] including consideration of the information and warnings given to subjects and the suitability, facilities and practice of the investigator. Reliance could therefore be placed on the regulatory character of such functions. On the other hand, as paragraph 1.2 of the GCP guidelines states, the primary responsibility for research, including design, conduct, obtaining consent and explaining risks, lies firmly with the investigator (and

*Definition—see page 28.

sponsor). Accordingly, it has been argued that legal responsibility should rest solely with the sponsor/investigator as long as a committee is not positively advocating a course of action but rather deciding whether or not a given proposal is to be within ethical bounds.[46] This view is strengthened by the approach taken in the 1991 DoH Guidelines that the function of ethics committees is purely advisory and that the responsibility for the decision rests with the NHS body under the auspices of which the research is to take place.

Pending a decision on this issue by the courts, the matter is open to speculation. At least members of an ethics committee should be in no worse a position than a regulatory authority. Settlement of the human immunodeficiency virus (HIV) haemophiliac litigation has pre-empted a judicial decision in the UK on whether a regulatory authority owes a duty of care to individuals who use a licensed or research product. The English Court of Appeal did hold in that litigation, on preliminary consideration of the point, that there is 'at least a good arguable claim in law based on common law negligence' although it was not required on that occasion to consider the point in further detail.[47] On the other hand, it has recently been held by the Privy Council that a banking regulatory authority did not have a duty of care to individual investors in exercising typical functions of modern government in the general public interest.[48]

## Conclusion

The establishment of the principles of Good Clinical Practice on a European-wide basis is an initiative by the CPMP which is very much to be welcomed. GCP is founded on sound principles of ethics, safety and quality. Inevitably, some interesting legal issues arise which will merit further consideration when GCP is enacted into national legislation. In the UK, it would be helpful for the implementing legislation to follow the French example of establishing ethics committees on a uniform basis throughout the country, specifying standardised provisions for constitutions, membership, procedures and documentation. This should assist the speedy and smooth operation of such committees, and result in benefits for the pharmaceutical industry, researchers, administrators and, above all, volunteer subjects.

## References

1.  Partner, Pharmaceutical and Healthcare Group, McKenna & Co., Solicitors, London; Member of the Advisory Board, *World Pharmaceutical Standards Review*; Member, Ethics Committee, Harrow Health

District at Northwick Park Hospital and the Medical Research Council's Research Centre.

2. Declaration of Helsinki approved by the 18th World Medical Assembly in Helsinki, Finland, 1964, and amended in Tokyo, Japan, 1975, Venice, Italy, 1983 and Hong Kong, 1989.
3. Federal Register, Vol. 46, No. 17, Tuesday, January 27, 1981.
4. The Medicines (Exemption from Licences) (Clinical Trials) Order 1981, SI 1981 No. 164 and MAL 62: Clinical trial exemption scheme.
5. German Drug Law 1976, Sections 40–42.
6. Republic of Ireland: Control of Clinical Trials Act, 1987; and Control of Clinical Trials and Drugs Act, 1990; France: Law on the Protection of Persons undergoing Biomedical Research, 1987, 1990, 1991.
7. Ley del Medicamento 25/1990, Third Title.
8. Directive 65/65/EEC Article 4(8); Directive 75/318/EEC Annex Part 3.
9. Recommended Basis for the Conduct of Clinical Trials of Medicinal Products in the European Community III/411/87-EN Rev.
10. Draft Directive III/9062/90-EN.
11. Good Clinical Practice for Trials on Medicinal Products in the European Community III/3976/88-EN Final, Paragraph 1.4.
12. *Ibid*, Paragraph 1.6(a).
13. *Research involving patients*, Royal College of Physicians, 1990, paragraphs 8.7, 10.9, 10.10.
14. France: Law on the Protection of Persons undergoing Biomedical Research, 1988, 1990, 1991; Republic of Ireland: Control of Clinical Trials Act, 1987, 1990; Spain: Medicaments Law 1990.
15. Responsibility in investigations on human subjects, MRC Annual Report 1982–83; Supervision of the Ethics of Clinical Research Investigations, Report of the Royal College of Physicians, 1972; DHSS Circular. Supervision of the Ethics of Clinical Research Investigations and Foetal Research, HSC (IS) 153, 1975.
15a. Health Service Guidelines: Circular HSG (91)5 and booklet. *Local Research Ethics Committees*, August 1991.
16. Advisory committees for the protection of persons undergoing biomedical research II—Code of Public Health, Book IIa, Title I.
17. Control of Clinical Trials Act, 1987, Section 8(1).
18. Control of Clinical Trials Act, 1987, Section 8(5).
19. Ley del Medicamento 25/1990, Title Three, Article 64.3.
20. Health Service Guidelines, *supra*, Paragraph 2.12.
21. Control of Clinical Trials Act, 1987, Section 4; Law on the protection of persons undergoing biomedical research, Article L.209-12; Ley del Medicamento 25/1990, Article 65.
22. Ley del Medicamento 25/1990, Article 60.
23. Ley del Medicamento 25/1990, Article 65.
24. *Freeman v. Home Office* (No. 2) [1984] Q.B. 524.
25. *Sidaway v. Bethlem Royal Hospital Governors* [1985] A.C. 871, H.L. applying *Bolam v. Friern Hospital Management Committee* [1957] 2 All ER 118, H.L.
26. Good Clinical Practice, *supra*, Paragraphs 1.8–1.15.
27. *Ibid*, Paragraph 1.14.
28. German Federal Drug Law 1976, Sections 1, 2, 84–94.
29. Health Circular: Good clinical practice, *supra*, Paragraph 1.6(e).

30. *Guidelines on the practice of ethics committees in medical research involving human subjects*, Report of the Royal College of Physicians of London, 1990.
31. Health Service Guidelines, *supra*, Paragraph 3.17.
32. *Guidelines on the practice of ethics committees, supra*, Paragraph 16.26.
33. German Drug Law 1976, Section 40.
34. French Decree no. 91-440 of 14 May 1991.
35. Irish Control of Clinical Trials Act 1987, Section 10 as amended.
36. Irish Control of Clinical Trials and Drugs Act, 1990, Section 3, amending Section 10 of the 1987 Act.
37. Ley del Medicamento 25/1990, Article 62.
38. French Law on the Protection of Persons undergoing Biomedical Research, Article L.209-7.
39. *Research on healthy volunteers*, Report of the Royal College of Physicians, 1986, page 11.
40. *Research involving patients, supra*, Chapter 11.7–11.10.
41. *Research involving patients, supra*, Chapter 11.6.
42. *Guidelines on the practice of ethics committees, supra*, Paragraph 16.25.
43. Good Clinical Practice, *supra*, paragraph 2.3(j).
44. Control of Clinical Trials and Drugs Act 1990, Section 5.
45. *Guidelines on the practice of ethics committees, supra*, Section 2.4.
46. Margaret Puxon QC. *Bulletin of Medical Ethics*, December 1990, p4.
47. re *HIV Haemophilia Litigation*, judgment of the Court of Appeal, 20 September 1990.
48. *Davis v. Radcliffe* [1990] 2 All ER 536.

## DISCUSSION

**Prof J. Thomson**: Insurance was mentioned towards the end of your presentation. Can you give us some idea of the scale of the problem: how many people who voluntarily undertook experimentation have suffered as a result?

**Mr Hodges**: As far as I know, there have been only two deaths within Europe (both in the 1980s). One was in Ireland, where there was a big public outcry which led to the Irish Act. The other was in Wales, I believe a student who did not disclose various facts about his medical history. I am not sure about other statistics, but the general safety record is known to be extremely good.

**Mr I. Dodds-Smith**: John Griffin[1] wrote a paper not long ago in which he presented some statistics on trials, and the percentage of people participating in them who were injured was very small. Despite so much attention being given to it, it is not a significant problem.

**Dame Rosalinde Hurley**: A similar paper was written by Jennifer Royle and Eric Snell.[2]

**Mr A.C. Osborn**: Are there any guidelines or rules concerning compensation relating to injury that is trial-related but not drug-related, and do sponsors have any obligations, for example, where an existing drug may be stopped in a run-in period and the patient then suffers an injury as a result?

**Mr Hodges**: This is addressed in the ABPI's latest guidelines. Injuries arising both in clinical trials to people taking placebos and in similar non-drug/procedure-related circumstances are generally not covered there. This brings us back to the matter of causation in general, that the plaintiff has to prove that the drug or another active intervention caused the injury whether under the guidelines or the general law.

### References

1. Spiers, C.J., Griffin, J. (1983). A survey of the first of the operation of the new procedure affecting the conduct of clinical trials in the United Kingdom. *Br J Clin Pharmacol* **15**, 649–55.
2. Royle, J.M., Snell, E.S. (1986). Medical research on normal volunteers. *Br J Clin Pharmacol*, **21**, 548–9.

# 7 | The basis of liability of the licensing authority and its advisers under the Medicines Act 1968 to an individual

**Anthony Barton**
*McKenna & Co, Solicitors, London*

## Introduction

In several recent multiclaimant actions in respect of medicinal products the licensing authority and the Committee on Safety of Medicines (CSM) have been joined as defendants. Such cases include the Opren and the blood product/haemophiliac litigation. The Opren cases concerned allegations that various reactions, including photodermatitis, were caused by the product, a non-steroidal anti-inflammatory agent. The haemophiliac litigation concerned allegations that haemophiliacs contracted human immunodeficiency virus (HIV) infection as a result of receiving contaminated blood products. The licensing authority was necessarily sued in respect of the exercise of its regulatory function under statute rather than in respect of any act or omission directly affecting the claimant. The CSM was sued in respect of its advice to the authority. The question of the liability of the licensing authority and the Committee, both public bodies, has thus been raised, but remains yet to be determined by the courts. This chapter explores the basis of such liability in the context of recent developments in the law of tort.

## The law

Increasingly, the adjudication of the courts is sought to determine questions concerning allegedly wrongful acts committed by public bodies. The same courts apply the same system of law whether the alleged wrongdoer is an individual or a public body because our legal system does not expressly distinguish between public and private law. Whilst our law is consistent with the maxim *'ubi ius, ibi remedium'* (where there is a right, there is a remedy), the classification of our law has been concerned more with remedies than with rights. This is a paradox which has caused much difficulty when individuals seek

91

redress in the courts against public bodies. It is the infringement of rights which may be protected either by public or by private law remedies that by implication gives rise to the distinction between public and private law. The public law remedy is judicial review; the private law remedy is an ordinary action for damages, sometimes supplemented by equitable relief. The two are mutually exclusive and provide entirely different sorts of relief. They may both, however, be concurrently applicable to the same alleged wrong because private law rights exist in parallel with public law rights. This difficulty has been recognised:

> ... the [ ] authority is a public body, discharging functions under statute: its powers and duties are definable in terms of public not private law. The problem which this type of action creates, is to define the circumstances in which the law should impose, over and above, or perhaps alongside these public law powers and duties, a duty in private law towards individuals such that they may sue for damages in a civil court. (per Lord Wilberforce, *Anns v. Merton London Borough Council* [1978] AC 728 at p.754).

Thus, the remedies sought in respect of a single wrongful act may be obtained by different procedures in parallel, depending upon the relief sought. To seek to obtain relief by the inappropriate remedy is, in general terms, deemed to be an abuse of the process of the court (*O'Reilly v. Mackman* [1983] 2AC 237). However, it is often not obvious which sort of remedy is appropriate to obtain relief. In certain cases, plaintiffs have sought compensation for grievances against public bodies by public law remedies, and it was held that private law remedies by ordinary action were appropriate (see *Davey v. Spelthorne Borough Council* [1984] AC 262; *R. v. East Berkshire Health Authority ex parte Walsh* [1985] QB 152; *Roy v. Kensington and Chelsea and Westminster Family Practitioner Committee, The Times* 27 March 1990).

In determining questions where the act of a public body has allegedly harmed an individual, the courts have considered the legal character of the act rather than enquire whether a public or private law right has been infringed. The court attempts to determine whether the act is policy (i.e. exercise of discretion, judicial, quasi-judicial) or operational (i.e. executive, administrative, business):

> Most, indeed probably all, statutes relating to public authorities or public bodies, contain in them a large area of policy. The courts call this 'discretion', meaning the decision is one for the authority or body to make, and not for the courts. Many statutes also prescribe or at least presuppose the practical execution of policy decisions: a convenient description is to say that in addition to the area of policy or discretion, there is an operational area. Although this distinction between the policy

area and the operational area is convenient, and illuminating, it is probably a distinction of degree; many 'operational' powers or duties have in them some element of 'discretion'. It can safely be said that the more 'operational' a power or duty may be, the easier it is to superimpose upon it a common law duty of care. (per Lord Wilberforce in *Anns v. Merton* at p.754).

In simple terms, policy acts give rise to public law rights, and their legality is tested by judicial review; operational acts give rise to private law rights, and their legality is tested by ordinary action. Thus, the lawful exercise of discretion does not give rise to private law rights. The underlying reason for this apparent immunity seems to be that the imposition of such liability would interfere with the exercise of discretion; such objections do not arise in respect of operational acts. This immunity, however, is not absolute because the exercise of discretion must be lawful. The exercise of discretion, tested by judicial review, is found to be unlawful where it is *ultra vires* (i.e. outside or in excess of powers), *mala fide* (i.e. in bad faith), or 'Wednesbury' unreasonable (i.e. so perverse that as a matter of law no reasonable tribunal could have arrived at such a decision).

The needs of modern society for a remedy where there has been loss caused to an individual by a public body have been considered by the courts:

> . . . over the past century the public law concept of *ultra vires* has replaced the civil law concept of negligence as the test of the legality, and consequently of the actionability, of acts or omissions of government departments or public authorities done in the exercise of a discretion conferred upon them by Parliament as to the means by which they are to achieve a particular public purpose. According to this concept Parliament has entrusted to the department or authority charged with the administration of the statute the exclusive right to determine the particular means within the limits laid down by the statute by which its purpose can best be fulfilled. It is not the function of the court, for which it would be ill-suited, to substitute its own view of the appropriate means for that of the department or authority by granting a remedy by way of a civil action at law to a private citizen adversely affected by the way in which the discretion has been exercised. Its function is confined in the first instance to deciding whether the act or omission complained of fell within the statutory limits imposed upon the department's or authority's discretion. Only if it did not would the court have jurisdiction to determine whether or not the act or omission, not being justified by the statute, constituted an actionable infringement of the plaintiff's rights in civil law. (per Lord Diplock in *Dorset Yacht Co. v. Home Office* (HL) [1970] AC 1004 at p. 1067).

This sort of reasoning was applied in the pertussis vaccination case of Kinnear (*Department of Health and Social Security v. Kinnear and others,*

*The Times*, 7 July 1984). In that case, it was held that the bona fide exercise of discretion in respect of an act of policy nature and within the lawful limits of discretion could not give rise to a cause of action.

The recovery of damages by an individual from a public body for an alleged wrongful act in the exercise of its discretion therefore requires the demonstration of unlawfulness under a two-stage test: unlawfulness at public law (*ultra vires*, *mala fides* or 'Wednesbury' unreasonableness) must be a condition precedent to actionability in private law. In the haemophiliac litigation, the plaintiffs claimed damages by alleging a breach of statutory duty in terms of unreasonableness, by which they sought to fulfil the condition precedent of unlawfulness at public law to permit actionability in private law.

The value of this dichotomy between policy and operation, however, in determining the incidence of liability in private law has been questioned:

> Their Lordships feel considerable sympathy with [his] difficulty in solving the problem by simple reference to this distinction. They are well aware of the references in the literature to this distinction . . . and of the critical analysis to which it has been subjected. They incline to the opinion, expressed in the literature, that this distinction does not provide a touchstone of liability, but rather is expressive of the need to exclude altogether those cases in which the decision under attack is of such a kind that a question whether it has been made negligently is unsuitable for judicial resolution . . . (per Lord Keith in *Rowling v. Takaro Properties Ltd.* (PC) [1988] AC 473 at p.501).

This distinction is crucial, however difficult its application. Such difficulties have arisen from the pragmatic concerns of our system of common law with remedies rather than rights.

### Public or private law?

In the usual case, the individual seeks compensation for loss arising from the alleged failure of a licensing authority exercising its duties and powers in accordance with the Medicines Act 1968. The individual does not seek to reverse the decision of a public body or question the legality of that decision, nor does the individual seek to question the powers of the licensing authority. Indeed, the claim for compensation depends upon the consequential loss arising from an incorrect decision. The Act, a statute largely concerned with public law, duties and powers, acknowledges the co-existence of private law rights but does not add to or subtract from them. Section 133(2) provides:

> . . . the provisions of this Act shall not be construed as –
>
>    (a) conferring a right of action in any civil proceedings (other than proceedings for the recovery of a fine) in respect of any contra-

vention of this Act or of any regulations or order made under this Act, or

(b) affecting any restriction imposed by or under any other enactment, whether contained in a public general Act or in a local or private Act, or

(c) derogating from any right of action or other remedy (whether civil or criminal) in proceedings instituted otherwise than under this Act.

It is appropriate, therefore, to seek compensatory damages by ordinary action in tort, and the options in tort need to be considered.

## Tort

### *Misfeasance*

This tort concerns the abuse of public office by a public officer in the discharge of his public duties. To constitute this tort the defendants must be shown to have acted with malice or with knowledge of the invalidity of their action. Plaintiffs have attempted unsuccessfully to proceed against public bodies by this action (*Dunlop v. Woollahra Municipal Council (PC)* [1982] AC 158; *Bourgoin SA v. Ministry of Agriculture Fisheries and Food* (CA) [1986] 1 QB 716). There is usually little to suggest, prima facie, that the licensing authority has acted out of malice or knowingly approved an invalid decision in the general case. Accordingly, an action for misfeasance will usually be fraught with difficulties.

### *Breach of statutory duty*

Public bodies often perform statutory duties under statutory power. To succeed by ordinary action in a claim for damages for breach of statutory duty it is necessary to identify whether there exists any statutory provision the express purpose of which is to protect the individual from the mischief complained of for which there is no statutory remedy:

> . . . . where a statute provides for the performance by certain persons of a particular duty, and some one belonging to a class of persons for whose benefit and protection the statute imposes the duty is injured by failure to perform it, prima facie, and, if there be nothing to the contrary, an action by the person so injured will lie against the person who has failed to perform the duty. (per Vaughan Williams LJ, *Groves v. Wimborne* [1898] 2 QB 402 at p.415).

It is arguable that there are such provisions in the Medicines Act 1968, imposing such a duty as to protect the individual, whether as a member of the class of patients or as a member of the public at large. However, the provisions of section 133(2) (supra) expressly deny such a duty as conferring a right of action.

## Negligence

It is trite law that a successful claim in negligence requires the establishing of the following elements:

1. The existence of a duty of care.
2. Breach of the duty of care.
3. Causation of loss/damage.
4. Loss/damage that is not too remote in law.

Whilst Lord Atkin's famous dictum in *Donoghue v. Stevenson* [1932] AC 562 is the source of the modern law of negligence, it has always been regarded as a guiding principle rather than a statement of law. The general retreat from the expansion of liability in negligence is applied by limiting these various elements. Because of the present general uncertain state of the law of negligence it is helpful to consider liability from first principles.

### *Duty of care*

It is useful to reconsider the actual words of Lord Atkin's dictum:

> You must take reasonable care to avoid acts or omissions which you can reasonably foresee would be likely to injure your neighbour. Who, then, in law is my neighbour? The answer appears to be—persons who are so closely and directly affected by my act that I ought reasonably to have them in contemplation as being so affected when I am directing my mind to the acts or omissions which are called in question. (*Donoghue v. Stevenson* at p.580)

This is the enunciation of the 'neighbour' principle and the related concept of 'proximity' which is formulated in terms of 'foreseeability'. Previously, this was considered to be a general principle which established a prima facie duty of care. It would then be necessary:

> . . . to consider whether there are any other considerations which ought to negative, or to reduce or limit the scope of the duty or the class of persons to whom it is owed or the damages to which a breach of it may give rise. (per Lord Wilberforce, *Anns v. Merton London Borough Council* at p.752).

This is the so-called 'two-stage' test. The courts no longer approve this approach. Foreseeability of harm is considered to be one circumstance to be taken into account. All the circumstances must be considered, and these include 'proximity', 'special relationship', 'fairness' and 'reasonableness'. The new position has been recently stated:

> . . . A series of decisions of the Privy Council and of your Lordships' House . . . have emphasised the inability of any single general principle to provide a practical test which can be applied to every situation to determine whether a duty of care is owed and, if so, what is its scope: . . . . What emerges is that, in addition to the foreseeability of damage, necessary ingredients in any situation giving rise to a duty of care are that there should exist between a party owing the duty and the party to whom it is owed a relationship characterised by the law as one of 'proximity' or 'neighbourhood' and that the situation should be one in which the court considered it is fair, just and reasonable that the law should impose a duty of a given scope on the one party for the benefit of the other. But it is implicit . . . that the concepts of proximity and fairness embodied in these additional ingredients are not susceptible of any such precise definitions as would be necessary to give them utility as practical tests, but amount in effect to little more than convenient labels to attach to the features of different specific situations which, on a detailed examination of all the circumstances, the law recognises pragmatically as giving rise to a duty of care of a given scope. Whilst recognising, of course, the importance of the underlying general principles common to the whole field of negligence, I think the law has moved in the direction of attaching greater significance to the more traditional categorisation of distinct and recognisable situations as guides to the existence, the scope and the limits of the varied duties of care which the law imposes. (per Lord Bridge in *Caparo Industries plc v. Dickman* [1990] 1 All ER 568 at p.573).

The liability in negligence of public bodies such as licensing, regulatory, or planning authorities to the individual has been examined recently in numerous cases; the cases fall into two broad categories:

1. Where the public body has affected the plaintiff directly by its alleged wrong.
2. Where the public body is alleged to have been negligent in the regulation or licensing or approval of the act of a third party which has caused damage to the plaintiff.

The liability of the licensing authority to an individual in respect of a medicinal product falls into the second category. These cases present a novel development in the law of negligence:

> As any proposition which relates to the duty of controlling another man to prevent his doing damage to a third deals with the category of civil wrongs of which the English courts have hitherto had little experience it would not be consistent with the methodology of the development of the law by judicial decision that any new proposition should be stated in wider terms than are necessary for the determination of the present appeal. Public policy may call for the immediate recognition of a new

sub-category of relations which are the source of a duty of this nature additional to the sub-category described in the established proposition, but further experience of actual cases would be needed before the time became ripe for the coalescence of sub-categories into a broader category of relations giving rise to the duty, such as was effected with respect to the duty of care of a manufacturer of products in *Donoghue v. Stevenson* . . . Nevertheless, any new sub-category will form part of the English law of civil wrongs and must be consistent with its general principles. (per Lord Diplock in *Dorset Yacht Co. v. Home Office* at p.1064).

Twenty years of further experience of actual cases has provided little assistance in determining such cases and indeed the courts now approve a piecemeal approach rather than a coalescence. Some assistance as to whether a duty of care is owed by a public authority may be provided by consideration of the statute by which the authority derives its duties and powers. This is the so-called 'statutory purpose' test (*Dutton v. Bognor Regis UDC*, [1972] 1 QB 373; *Anns v. Merton, Governors of the Peabody Donation Fund v. Sir Lindsey Parkinson Ltd*, [1985] AC 210).

> The purpose for which the powers . . . have been conferred on the [public body] is not to safeguard [the plaintiffs] against economic loss resulting from their failure to comply . . . . It is in my opinion to safeguard the occupiers of houses . . . and also members of the public generally, against dangers to their health. . . . (per Lord Keith in *Peabody* at p.241).

Thus, in determining the justice and fairness of imposing a duty of care, the court examines, *inter alia*, the statutory purpose for which the public body derives its authority. The powers, duties and the intended class to be protected are considered. The nature of the duty allegedly breached would have to be closely related to the purpose of the power. The statutory purpose of the Medicines Act 1968 has been judicially considered:

> The licensing authority are advised by experts in the field of medicinal products. The information available to the licensing authority consists of the knowledge obtained by these experts based on long experience, the information in published literature and, over the years, the vast amount of information provided by large numbers of applicants for product licences . . . . The principal task of the licensing authority is to protect the public . . . . The licensing authority cannot discharge its duty to safeguard the health of the nation . . . . without having recourse to all the information available to the licensing authority . . . when carrying out any function imposed upon the licensing authority by the Act of 1968 in the interests of the public. (per Lord Templeman, *Regina v. Licensing Authority, Ex parte Smith Kline, (HL)* [1990] 1 AC 64 at p.103).

The Council of the European Community has promulgated a Directive (65/65 EEC) on the approximation of provisions laid down by law, regulation or administrative action relating to proprietary and medicinal products. The provisions of this Directive, as amended and amplified from time to time by subsequent Directives, became binding on the UK on 1 January 1973, and must be performed and observed by the licensing authority. The Directive of 1965 recited, *inter alia*:

> ... the primary purpose of any rules concerning the production and distribution of proprietary medicinal products must be to safeguard public health; ...

The purpose of the Medicines Act 1968 appears consistent with this Directive. It seems that the statutory purpose of the Act is, in broad terms, concerned with the safety and licensing of medicinal products. A duty of care, by this test, would appear to be owed to the class of patients as a whole rather than individually.

Recently, the courts have demonstrated the new conservative and restrictive approach in imposing a duty of care on public bodies. It is regarded as undesirable for a public body exercising its typical functions of government in the general public interest to be liable to an unnamed, unidentified and smaller class of the public in failing adequately to regulate wrongful acts of a third party. Furthermore, the degree of control of the government body over the third party must be related to the duty owed. Generally, in respect of government bodies, such control is usually not sufficient to give rise to liability. If such liability were desirable on policy grounds, the court has indicated that it is a matter for the legislature, which is better suited than the judiciary to weigh up competing policy considerations (*Hill v. Chief Constable of West Yorkshire* (CA) [1988] 1 QBD 60; *Yuen Kun Yeu v. A.G. of Hong Kong* (PC) [1988] AC 175; *Davies v. Radcliffe* (PC) [1990] 2 All ER 563).

> It is at this stage that it is necessary, before concluding that a duty of care should be imposed, to consider all the relevant circumstances. One of the considerations ... is the fear that a too literal application of a well-known observation of Lord Wilberforce in *Anns v. Merton London Borough Council* ..., may be productive of a failure to have regard to, and to analyse and weigh, all the relevant considerations in considering whether it is appropriate that a duty of care should be imposed. Their Lordships consider that question to be of an intensely pragmatic character, well suited for gradual development but requiring most careful analysis ...

> In all the circumstances, it must be a serious question for consideration whether it would be appropriate to impose liability in negligence in these cases, or whether it would not rather be in the public interest that citizens should be confined to their remedy, as at present, in those cases where the minister or public authority has acted in bad faith. (per Lord Keith in *Rowling v. Takaro* p.501 and p.503).

More recently, the House of Lords has considered whether a public body owes a duty of care to an individual and, as the question was *obiter*, their Lordships were expressly silent:

> [There] may be cogent reasons of social policy for imposing liability on the authority. But the shoulders of a public body are only 'broad enough to bear loss' because they are financed by the public at large. It is pre-eminently for the legislature to decide whether these policy reasons should be accepted as sufficient for imposing on the public the burden of providing compensation for private financial losses. If they do so decide, it is not difficult for them to say so. (per Lord Bridge in *Murphy v. Brentwood District Court* (HL) [1990] 2 All ER 908 at p.931).

Although the case of alleged negligence by the licensing authority for medicinal products has not been tested in the courts, consideration of previous cases indicates their reluctance to create a new category of liability and that, in any case, the balance of interest would fall such that the public interest is favoured rather than the individual interest.

Most recently, the liability of government bodies was considered in *re Haemophiliac Litigation*, (Court of Appeal, 20 September 1990). The defendants included the Department of Health, the licensing authority and the CSM. The matters before the court mainly concerned discovery issues against the Department of Health. The question arose as to the validity of the causes of action, namely negligence and breach of statutory duty. It was considered that the plaintiffs had 'made out at least a good arguable claim in law based upon common law negligence'. Dicta suggest that this term was not to be taken to be an indication of the merits of the plaintiffs' claim, but rather that as a matter of law a minimum threshold had been achieved.

### Breach of duty of care

Breach of duty is a mixed question of law and fact, and its determination requires factual investigation. The licensing authority under the Medicines Act 1968 is responsible for the grant, renewal, variation, suspension and revocation of licences and certificates (Section 6). It is a body of ministers consisting of, *inter alia*, the 'health ministers'. The CSM was established to 'give advice with respect to safety, quality or efficacy' of medicines and to promote 'the collection and investigation of information relating to adverse reactions for the purpose of enabling such advice to be given' (Section 4). Where a body has been professionally advised in reaching a decision, it is able to delegate that duty and reasonably discharge that duty thereby (*Dunlop v. Woollahra Municipal Council*). Presumably, such is the position where the licensing authority has been advised by the CSM. The delegation is of itself reasonable, and the reliance upon the Committee's advice will be difficult to characterise as negligent. Furthermore, there may be semantic difficulties in finding a body such as the CSM to be in breach of duty. Under the 'Bolam' test, an act is deemed not to be negligent if it is consistent with a recognised but minority body of responsible medical opinion (*Bolam v. Friern Hospital Management Committee* [1957] 2 All ER 118). By its very composition, the CSM is such a responsible body of medical opinion. For this reason, a claim in negligence against its members will face fundamental difficulties.

*Causation*

Causation is a pure question of fact involving application of the 'but for' test. Legal causation is determined thus: but for the act complained of, would the loss have occurred? In medical litigation it is the proof of causation, above all, which may cause greatest difficulty to a plaintiff. The courts have shown a reversion to the rigorous application of the 'but for' test (*Wilsher v. Essex Area Health Authority* (HL) [1988] AC 1074).

*Remoteness of damage in law*

The courts have recently reasserted the principle that for damages to be recoverable in negligence it must be related to physical injury (*Murphy v. Brentwood District Council*). Medical litigation cases by their very nature involve personal injury, and this restriction does not generally present a difficulty. However, where a pharmaceutical company seeks damages for the wrong decision of the licensing authority, such loss as it has suffered can usually be formulated only in terms of economic loss. Accordingly, the recovery of such loss is likely to be difficult.

## Conclusions

To succeed against the licensing authority for medicinal products and its advisers, the individual must proceed by ordinary action for damages. The tort of negligence is the appropriate action. Difficulties arise in establishing that a duty of care is owed by a public body to an individual. Establishing a breach of that duty is a question of fact which requires investigation. This may be difficult under the 'Bolam' test, for the CSM is itself a responsible body of medical opinion. Causation in medical litigation is often extremely difficult and the test is strictly applied. The present conservative and restrictive approach of the courts when considering the liability of government bodies in negligence may endow such bodies with a sort of substantive immunity. A duty is owed not to individuals but to the public at large, and such an unnamed, unnumbered class cannot, of course, proceed by ordinary action. The recent cases have been settled. Commercial and political expediency may have been considerations as much as the merits and the law. As the system of medical litigation and compensation is constantly under review this question may well remain unanswered by the courts.

# 8 | Unlicensed medicines and the use of drugs in unlicensed indications

**Ronald D. Mann**

*Medical Services Secretary, Royal Society of Medicine, London*
*Director, VAMP Research Ltd, London*

## Introduction

The licensing system shares the responsibility for the initial assessment and continuing review of the benefit/risk ratio of a medicine. The use of an unlicensed medicine, or the use of a medicine outside the terms of the licensed indications in the data sheet, almost always places the weight of responsibility on the individual practitioner and company concerned. It must be assumed, therefore, to increase the exposure to legal liability of those involved,[1,2] and this is especially so now that the Product Liability Directive (EEC/85/374) is in place in Europe and has been carried into UK law in the form of the Consumer Protection Act 1987.

## The licensing provisions

*The Medicines Act 1968*

Section 7(2) of the Medicines Act provides (amongst other things) that no person 'in the course of a business carried on by him . . .' shall sell, supply or export any medicinal product except in accordance with a product licence. The Act also controls the importation of medicines (Section 7(3)), their manufacture and wholesale dealing in them (Section 8), and their use in clinical trials, for which a product licence, clinical trial certificate (Section 31(3)), or clinical trial certificate exemption (S.I. 1981, No. 164), is required if a commercially interested party is involved.

The general effect is to regulate closely the activities of pharmaceutical companies and those concerned, by way of business, with the provision of medicines. However, the Act does not aim to restrict the clinical judgement of individual medical practitioners, and therefore contains important exemptions for doctors, dentists, veterinary surgeons (Section 9), pharmacists (Section 10), and nurses and midwives (Section 11). It also has exemptions relating to the use of herbal remedies (Section 12).

Doctors are free to prescribe unlicensed medicinal products and can advise medicines for uses or in doses or by routes of administration outside the authorised recommendations given in the data sheets of licensed medicinal products. They can allow their judgement to override the warnings and precautions given in the data sheets — but they do all these things on their personal professional responsibility. In increasingly litigious times, a real concern for the medical or dental practitioner is that he may incur civil liability in tort to a patient who has been injured following prescription of an unlicensed medicine. The doctor who uses unlicensed medicines or prescribed drugs in unlicensed indications needs to question himself closely and ensure not only that he is adopting a practice in so prescribing that would be endorsed by a responsible body of professional opinion (the test for discharge of the duty of care) but also that he has (other than in exceptional circumstances) the valid consent of a fully informed patient. He would, it seems clear, be wise to record this consent.

Section 9(1) of the Medicines Act contains provisions which exempt the doctor or dentist from having to obtain a product or manufacturing licence under the requirements of Sections 7 and 8 in respect of anything done '. . . which relates to a medicinal product specially prepared, or specially imported by him or to his order, for administration to a particular patient of his . . .'. This reference to 'a particular patient' seems to be the basis of the concept of the 'named patient' which has arisen and persisted in some quarters. Some pharmaceutical companies keep records of the names of all patients whose doctors have been supplied, on their request, with unlicensed medicines. These exemptions from the normal licensing requirements are consistent with European law as set out in Directive 65/65/EEC (see below).

The Section 9 exemptions cover doctors doing things at the request of another doctor when particular patients of that other doctor are concerned. The exemptions were further widened by S.I. 1972, No. 1200, so that a doctor does not need a product licence to procure the manufacture of a limited stock of an unlicensed product with the idea that the medicine will be administered to one or more patients of his, or of other doctors in his group, provided that the manufacturer of the medicine holds a 'special licence'. The manufacturer must hold a manufacturer's licence which has been extended by the licensing authority to allow provision of these special services. From the point of view of the manufacturer, S.I. 1971, No. 1450 imposes specific conditions, in particular that orders for products to be supplied under these arrangements must be unsolicited. The companies concerned are most unwise even to provide a brochure of the products they make under their 'special licence'. There are companies and branches of medicine in which rather extensive use is made of the named patient and special provisions. It is, perhaps, in respect of such activities that circumvention of the need to obtain a product licence can most readily arise, and some concern can properly be expressed as to the lack of review implicit in the product licence arrangements.

## Importing of unlicensed medicines

Unlicensed medicines are sometimes imported for patients in the UK or for visitors from overseas. Section 13 of the Act allows import of a product by a doctor, company, or visitor without a product licence for his own use or for named patient supply as applicable. However, this automatic exemption does not allow the import of stock for as yet unidentified patients. The Medicines (Exemption from Licences) (Importation) Order 1984 (S.I. 1984, No. 673) is relevant to this issue, and deserves to be widely known amongst doctors dealing with patients who need to use imported drugs unlicensed in the UK. Not only does this statutory instrument comprehend the exemption of Section 13 but it also allows the import of limited stock for named patient supply. Doctors need to note that there are complex requirements imposed on them if they take advantage of the provisions of S.I. 1984, No. 673; in particular, they must give notice to the licensing authority of intention to import. In practice, they are well advised to consult the Medicines Control Agency (MCA) of the Department of Health for guidance.

## Personal clinical investigations

Doctors sometimes wish to conduct personal clinical investigations undertaken on their own initiative and in which a pharmaceutical company is not involved. If a company is initiating the study, then a product licence, a clinical trial certificate or a clinical trial certificate exemption must be obtained. Doctors should never agree to pretend that the idea of undertaking a study began with them when it did not, because any such pretence will lead to false certification. Provided that the trial is not undertaken at the request of a third party, a doctor can take advantage of the extensive exemptions provided by S.I. 1972, No. 1200 (The Medicines (Exemption from Licences) (Special Cases and Miscellaneous Provisions) Order 1972) which has already been mentioned. The doctor must notify the licensing authority (in practice, the Medicines Control Agency of the Department of Health) giving details of the trial and the method of supply of the medicinal product to be used. He is claiming what is commonly known as a 'doctors' and dentists' exemption' and must wait 21 days (or any extended period of time notified to him) so that the licensing authority can raise objections if it wishes. Doctors contacting the agency are well advised to ask for the guidance leaflet MAL 31 and forms MLA 162 (which they complete) and MLA 163 (which the supplier of the medicinal product must complete). Ethical permission is, of course, an additional professional requirement, and doctors involved in setting up their own clinical trials may wish to consider obtaining no-fault compensation cover (commercial policies are available)[3] and ensure that their medical protection policy permits the proposed activity.

When taking part in trials in which companies or third parties are involved doctors should make certain that they have an up-to-date copy of the investigators' brochure, that they have studied it in relationship to the proposed protocol, and that ethical approval has been given and indemnity arrangements are in place.

### *The European Economic Community Directives*

The European Economic Community (EEC) Directives determine the requirements of national law, but they have confirmed the right to supply unlicensed products in appropriate circumstances. They do not prohibit doctors and dentists from prescribing outside the terms of the data sheet. Directive 89/341/EEC amends the earlier Directives (65/65/EEC; 75/319/EEC) and adds, by Article 1(3), the following wording to 65/65/EEC:

> A Member State may, in accordance with legislation in force and to fulfil special needs, exclude from Chapters II to V . . .

(ie from the licensing requirements)

> medicinal products supplied in response to a *bona fide* unsolicited order, formulated in accordance with the specifications of an authorised health care professional and for use by his individual patients on his direct personal responsibility.

These provisions are to be implemented by national law by January 1992, but already appear covered by UK medicines legislation, as described above. Once again, it will be noted that this wording makes it clear where the responsibility for using unlicensed medicines lies.

### **Types of unlicensed medicines**

From the medical point of view, unlicensed medicines include:
**1.** *Drugs in clinical trial.* Provided that there has been compliance with the regulatory requirements, approval of an ethics committee has been

obtained, and there is compliance with the appropriate published guidelines, the study of such drugs represents a normal part of the development of a medicine towards its product licence. A problem can, however, arise when, at the end of the study, the doctor wishes to continue use of the experimental drug in a patient who has benefited from it. In such circumstances, it is probably better to extend the formal trial rather than to resort to use of the unlicensed medicine on a 'named patient' basis. In any event, doctors would be wise to review carefully the altered ethical and legal positions, for the available animal safety evaluation and carcinogenicity data may not justify the longer period of human exposure envisaged. Where the doctor feels the need for further advice, he should consult his protection society.

**2.** *Medicines for which an earlier product licence has been abandoned or not renewed (often for commercial reasons) or has been suspended or revoked (often for safety reasons or because the data have been found to be inadequate upon review).* Clinical circumstances may make supply on a 'named patient' basis seem imperative but the use of alternative medicines is almost always to be preferred. If the 'named patient' route is chosen, it would seem essential that the exact circumstances are disclosed to the patient who should give recorded informed consent.

**3.** *Medicines which have never been licensed in this country.* A common type of unlicensed medicine is the medicinal product which is similar to a licensed product but is not itself licensed. Such drugs are often made under a 'specials licence'. They may be needed for individuals who are allergic to ingredients of the licensed preparation. Low-dose formulations for children or liquid preparations for the elderly form other examples of these variants on a licensed theme. Requests for active ingredients or for the manufacture of medicines which are licensed abroad are also fairly frequent. Companies and doctors involved in making and using unlicensed medicines of these kinds need, as always, to bear in mind their enhanced liability. Frank abuses of the licensing system can occur within these provisions, and a suitable licensed medicine should be introduced if possible. The dangers of altered bioavailability need to be kept in mind, and it is almost always better to secure the permission of the licensing authority to the importation of a medicine licensed abroad rather than make an extemporaneous variant of it.

It will be clear that the exemptions from licensing permitted by Section 9 of the Medicines Act are intended to enable doctors to deal with the needs of particular patients. The continued provision outside clinical trials of an unlicensed medicine to fairly substantial numbers of patients may well represent an evasion of the licensing requirements and is to be deprecated.

Examples of the difficulties which can arise are the extensive 'named patient' distribution which occurred with the then unlicensed drug oxybutynin used in the treatment of detrusor instability,[4] and the use of the licensed drug benzhexol in the unlicensed but important indication of dystonia.[5] Such situations are unsatisfactory for all concerned: prescribers have unwelcome legal and ethical exposure, and lack the protection implicit in the licensing system. Companies may wish ideally to supply only licensed drugs for licensed indications, but some products might not support the development, registration and distribution costs. It is likely that the helpful provisions of Directive 75/318/ EEC, Annex Part 3, Chapter III, Article 5, which, in effect, allows the licensing of 'orphan drugs' and 'orphan indications', have been much underused in these situations.[6]

## Practical implications

### Professional and product liability

In essence, there are two main legal regimes which permit an injured person to obtain compensation: negligence liability and strict liability. Negligence (or fault) liability is already very familiar to doctors, but the concept of strict liability (or liability without fault) introduces fairly new elements with which many doctors are unfamiliar.

Strict liability can arise from a contract or from the Product Liability Directive (85/374/EEC) and Consumer Protection Act 1987. In the UK strict liability can arise from the type of contract advocated by the *Guidelines for medical experiments in non-patient human volunteers*, issued by the Association of the British Pharmaceutical Industry. These contracts intentionally provide considerable protection for healthy human volunteers taking part in clinical studies which are outside the remit of the Medicines Act. The Sale of Goods legislation (the Sale of Goods Act 1979) can also imply conditions into contracts of sale: the seller of a medicinal product will be liable, independent of fault on his part, for injury suffered by the buyer if the product was not of adequate or 'merchantable' quality. However, the buyer–seller relationship is seldom relevant to the provision of prescription medicines for the courts have clearly declared that medicines supplied under the National Health Service are not supplied in pursuit of a contract between the patient and pharmacist.

A new and important development in relation to product liability is Directive 85/374/EEC, which states that 'the producer shall be liable for damage caused by a defect in his product' (Article 1); 'the injured person should be required to prove the damage, the defect and the causal relationship between defect and damage' (Article 4); and, 'a product is defective when it does not provide the safety which a person is entitled to expect, taking all circumstances into account . . .' (Article 6).

It will be apparent that the product can be considered defective on the basis of a consumer test—of what the patient is entitled to expect— and this test can be affected by the verbal and written information given to the patient and the warnings therein. Thus, a producer's (ie manufacturer's) 'failure to warn' that a medicinal product is unlicensed (and may, therefore, be less comprehensively reviewed in terms of its scientific data than a licensed product) would expose the 'producer' to risk of liability for injury. Unless the doctor or dentist has made the drug administered to a patient who suffers injury, or is responsible for the first importation of the product into the Community, strict liability is unlikely to apply. There are additional ways in which doctors, pharmacists and pharmaceutical companies can be subject to product liability, and it is important that those concerned should be familiar with the relevant provisions.

## Data limitations

The use of unlicensed products or of licensed products for unlicensed indications frequently occurs in response to individual papers in medical journals. Doctors need to realise that the database provided by even the best of such publications is very much less than the compilation of pharmaceutical, toxicological and clinical data submitted in support of a product licence application. The fact that those data which are available will normally not have been reviewed by a major drug regulatory agency with access to all the data on all marketed medicines is also important and needs to be explained to the patient concerned. Information on the adverse reaction profile of some unlicensed medicines is also usually grossly inadequate because there is no mechanism for these data to be assembled and made available to investigators. There is, in terms of patient safety, no substitute for the integrated database prepared by a research-based pharmaceutical company and submitted for independent review by the regulatory authorities.

## Labelling

The labelling regulations (S.I. 1976, No. 1726) in the UK do not require disclosure of the fact that there is no product licence number. A new EEC Directive on patient information is currently being de-

veloped, but its provisions will not affect the use of unlicensed medicines — an issue which perhaps needs further consideration.

## Summary

Doctors caring for particular patients can use unlicensed medicines
and can depart from the prescribing guidance given by the data sheet of
licensed medicines — but only on their personal professional responsibility. Recent changes in product liability legislation appear to have
increased the exposure to liability both of companies producing and of
doctors manufacturing or importing from outside the EEC unlicensed
medicinal products. There is, as yet, no relevant experience of the
working of the Consumer Protection Act 1987, but it would seem
advisable for doctors, having regard both to their liability for negligence and to the possibility in limited circumstances of liability under
this Act, to explain clearly to patients the nature and perceived risks
and benefits of unlicensed medicinal products, so that informed consent can be obtained and recorded. In addition, it seems appropriate
that doctors should take increased care to ensure that their practices
regarding such medicines comply with the requirements of the licensing authority as regards the conditions of exemption and are acceptable
to those responsible for their professional indemnity arrangements.

## References

1. Dodds-Smith I (1989). The implications of strict liability for medicinal
   products under the Consumer Protection Act 1987. In: *Risk and consent to
   risk in medicine* (Ed. RD Mann). Carnforth, Lancs: Parthenon, pp 107–31.
2. Mann RD (1990). The impact of product liability on the practice of
   medicine and clinical research: the viewpoint of a physician. *26th Annual
   Meeting of the Drug Information Association* (San Francisco, California;
   3–7 June 1990) (In press).
3. B & C Insurance Broking Group (undated). *No-fault compensation for
   clinical trials/volunteer studies*. London: B & C Ltd.
4. Anonymous (1988). Terodiline and oxybutynin in detrusor instability.
   *Drug and Therapeutics Bulletin* **26**(10), 37–8.
5. Anonymous (1988). Dystonia: underdiagnosed and undertreated? *Drug
   and Therapeutics Bulletin* **26**(9), 33–6.
6. Mann RD (1986). UK regulatory requirements for orphan drugs. In:
   *Orphan diseases and orphan drugs* (Ed. I Herbert Scheinberg and JM
   Walshe) Manchester: Manchester University Press, pp 146–9.

# 9 | Compensation for adverse consequences of medical intervention: a legal view of the Royal College of Physicians (London) report

**Colin Milne**

*Partner, Wright, Johnston & Mackenzie, Solicitors, Glasgow*

## Introduction

Normally, before any lawyer says or writes anything on any given subject he or she gives it full consideration, and what then is said or written usually comes across as carefully thought out and reasoned. That said, as with most people, lawyers approach any given subject with some preconceived ideas—which are seldom voiced. Mine were triggered by reading the first sentence of the President of the Royal College of Physicians (RCP) press statement:

> It is generally agreed that our current system of compensating those who suffer adverse consequences after medical intervention is far from satisfactory.

My first thought, 'not that old chestnut again', is untenable. Society is concerned about medical negligence claims. On 20 April 1991 in London I heard a speaker at a conference talk about medical negligence cases 'limping to court', and then go on to describe the current state of medical negligence claims as a 'major public scandal'. The speaker was neither an aggrieved victim nor a medical member of Militant Tendency (assuming there are such), but a judge of the High Court of Justice, Queen's Bench Division (Mr Justice Brooke).

My second thought was that if we are to debate no-fault again, why single out the medical profession? Society's concern about medical negligence claims is perhaps the reason. If there is any doubt about it, the fact that such matters are being debated in Parliament tells its own story. Indeed, in Hansard's report for 14 January 1991, reference is made to the RCP's Report—which, if nothing else, shows that the

111

College's hope that publication would be followed by a public debate
about the problem, as expressed in the press statement referred to
earlier, has been achieved.

My third thought was that it is not really a problem in Scotland
anyway, but the fact is that while there are differences between Scottish
and English law, medical negligence claims have had as bad a press in
Scotland as in England. For example, some years ago the *Kay v.
Ayrshire and Arran Health Board* case received a TV exposé by Jimmy
Reid (a well-known Scottish figure who first came into the public eye at
the time of the workers' sit-in at Upper Clyde Shipbuilders, but who
has since turned into a highly regarded TV investigative journalist).
His description of the way the legal system dealt with medical negligence claims certainly led to public concern about how such cases were
handled.

As with any report, the first item to consider is the membership of the
Working Party. Suffice to say that the list is impressive, and it is
therefore no surprise to find that the Report is of high quality.


## The Report

### Introduction and Chapter 1

Chapter 1 sets the scene. The College's concerns about the problems
raised for the practice of medicine are identified: sharp growth in the
frequency and severity of medical liability claims, the cost of insurance,
and the risk that doctors might practise what is called defensive
medicine rather than meeting the actual clinical needs of patients.
These considerations are, of course, proper as far as the medical
profession is concerned, but the College also recognises the growing
public anxiety about what seem to be inequities of the legal process of
establishing negligence. It also identifies from the start that the phrase
'no fault' covers a number of schemes, and it is therefore better to work
from first principles in looking at options rather than assume that there
is any magical 'no-fault' formula.

The terms of reference defined by the Working Party were as follows,
and seem perfectly appropriate:

(a) to consider the means of providing compensation and redress for
    people who have sustained some physical or psychological damage
    consequent upon an encounter with medical care;
(b) to investigate the efficiency and equity of the arrangements which
    currently exist in England and Wales, focusing particularly on the
    tort system;
(c) to evaluate the alternative compensation schemes which have been
    proposed or introduced in other countries, such as the no-fault

systems in New Zealand, Sweden and Finland, with particular regard to their administrative costs and their implications for medical accountability and standards of care; and

(d)  to make recommendations intended to improve the current position of injured patients.

### Chapter 2: Compensation under tort — causation, fault and quantum

This chapter offers a good summary of the present system which concisely explains the way things are and should lead to a greater understanding of how the issues work in practice; for example, the problems in causation, what negligence really means, and the way the courts assess the loss.

### Chapter 3: Evaluating the tort system

One might like to argue that this chapter, which offers the Working Party's evaluation of the present system, is controversial, but much of what is said is simply statements of fact. What is said about *delay, cost* and *quality of legal representation*, especially for the plaintiff, is all too true. I do not know whether or not what is said about *defensive practices* is true — it would certainly be difficult to prove.

More controversial in the evaluation are the allegations about *inequity both to patients and to defendants*. These allegations about inequity focus on the whole legal system. It is stated in relation to patients (quite correctly) that injured patients are treated differently, depending upon whether or not they can prove the causal connection between event and outcome. This is the central point of our fault system. If there are examples where a patient cannot prove fault and suffers loss — is it fair or not? This, surely, is a big issue for society to debate and the Report is quite right in bringing it to the forefront.

The point about inequity to defendants (ie doctors) is well made, but again this focuses on the whole legal system because any defendant runs the risk of public notice if the case actually comes to a hearing. It prompts what will prove to be my recurring theme: why should doctors be any different? It is a fact of life that any court case can attract publicity which, inevitably, focuses on the evidence given in court, particularly if it is of a sensational nature. The final judgement, even if it vindicates the defendant, does not always attract the same degree of publicity. The College is, however, right in seeking to have this issue debated publicly.

Finally, in relation to the evaluation of the present system, the issue of lump sum awards is raised. This is almost a separate topic in itself and deserves full public debate, given the inevitable consequences for insurers and health authorities.

*Chapter 4: Evaluating alternatives to tort*

This chapter offers an evaluation of alternatives to the present system. I think the evaluation is fair but, as might be expected, finance features prominently. The question of who pays is critical, whatever method is used to determine eligibility for compensation. The choices are identified as:

— the patient himself or his insurer;
— the doctor or his insurer;
— the doctor's employer or his insurer;
— the general taxpayer.

Finance inevitably is the underlying theme when it comes to a consideration of the options for reform.

*Chapter 5: Options for reform*

In terms of simply listing the options, the Report is comprehensive. The first option considered is the *status quo* or, more accurately, the *status quo* as it might be improved. Many of the current problems are linked to the delay that litigants experience in the court, and there is more than enough concern about it in other areas to justify substantial interest from many other sources to improve the present system. Indeed, in quoting Mr Justice Brooke earlier, I should perhaps explain that the context of that conference was a fairly high-powered look at the use of information technology in resolving court disputes. That the Lord Chancellor was the first speaker is an indication of the government's interest in this whole subject, but there is a lot more going on other than looking at information technology. There are reviews in England and Wales of the entire court system and in Scotland a consultation paper is already in place on the subject of court procedures. Procedures, however, are one thing; the resources to make procedures work is another and that will be the more difficult aspect to resolve.

The Report recognises the government's intentions with regard to reforming civil procedure, but questions whether or not that will improve the situation in relation to medical negligence. Improvements to the present system, however, presuppose that the present system is right. This has to be the main issue for debate here: is the present system right or is 'no fault' the answer?

The Report offers relevant background information on the patient insurance scheme set up in Sweden, and also gives some background to the New Zealand Accident Compensation Scheme. These schemes provide compensation for the patient, which can be claimed as of right without the claimant proving fault. The appeal of these schemes is, of course, that fault does not need to be established, but there are restrictions and limitations (which is to be expected with any scheme). Nothing is as simple as it first seems, since, inevitably, there are overall restrictions in terms of funding.

The Working Party then looked at general disability income, which superficially offers a very attractive alternative, doing away with proof of cause or fault perhaps more than any other option that poses major political issues in terms of funding.

*Chapter 6: Conclusions and recommendations*

By this time the reader has had the benefit of a comprehensive overview of the existing system and the other options. The Report correctly identifies the issues as being part of a more general debate about compensation policy, which prompts the question whether or not the provision of medical services should be treated any differently. The answer given in the Report is in the affirmative. I do not find their answer convincing, but at least I understand their arguments.

In their Conclusions, the Working Party considers that the present system is deficient as a means for providing compensation, and offers seven reasons for that statement:

— inequity to plaintiffs;
— delay;
— cost;
— quality of legal representation, particularly in relation to plaintiffs;
— inequity to defendants;
— lump sum awards, with their attendant problems for the unsophisticated plaintiff; and
— the possibility that doctors might adopt defensive practices.

I would have preferred the Working Party to expand on their reasons, but I suppose the mere statement of their reasons stimulates debate. Some of the reasons (delay, cost and perhaps quality of legal representation) are remediable by sharpening up the present system. The so-called 'inequity to plaintiffs' and 'inequity to defendants' raises a more fundamental point of the whole system which requires debate. I do not find these alleged inequities sufficient reason to conclude that the present system is deficient. In relation to the alleged inequity to plaintiffs, I would say that if society wishes to provide for plaintiffs differently in a no-fault system, whether by an extension of the social security system or something else, it will require a policy decision by government and for society to collaborate in making the resources available.

I support the conclusions in relation to the concern about delay, but believe the thrust there should be directed towards improving the present system. This is now universally accepted, and it is a question of all involved in the present system moving towards implementing steps that will lead to real progress.

Inequity to defendants does not seem to me to be a major issue. It is for the doctors involved to justify being treated differently from the rest of society, and I would be interested to hear their views; the Report does not expand on this point to any extent. I would also like to hear what the medical profession has to say about defensive practices. It may be difficult for them to justify this although one can see why there is concern. Lump sum awards are almost a separate, or side issue, and I am not convinced that this needs to be brought into the main area of debate.

Before turning to the Recommendations, the Working Party summarises the alternatives they considered, namely, *patient insurance*, *accident compensation* and *general disability income*. At the start of their recommendations they record their awareness, arising from consideration of these alternatives, that there will remain inequities in any no-fault scheme—the only permanent solution being implementation of a comprehensive disability income scheme—with all that involves politically and whether or not society would bear the cost. Recognising that this will not happen overnight, they recommend the introduction of a no-fault scheme with certain features, which involve the capping of economic damages (eg loss of earnings) and non-economic damages (eg pain and suffering). Unfortunately, the financial implications of introducing this scheme were not addressed. They may believe that public debate on the issue would lead to consideration of the financial implications, but I think the first question anyone will ask is how will this be financed. It is only by getting an answer to this question that a proper view can be expressed on the scheme. It might be thought desirable to establish the principle first and work out the details later, but if the abandoning of a system that is well established, despite current problems, is being suggested, all the issues have to be fully explored—all the more so because my view of the present system is that it can work if improvements are carried out. I accept that still leaves the underlying problems of how to compensate people where fault cannot be established, but I see it as a political issue with scope for introducing a new element of compensation on top of the present schemes.

The Working Party's recommendations for the introduction of a no-fault scheme envisage there being a choice between suing on negligence or adopting the scheme. For actions that continue to be brought on negligence it is recommended that certain procedural rules be reviewed. I find the first recommendation (that the court should be required to satisfy itself that evidence as to opinion is permitted only from the medical witnesses with appropriate expertise) almost unnecessary. It is for the court to assess the worth of any witness. It will not help to insist on some special qualification before someone can give evidence. I do, however, agree with the other principles, namely, full disclosure, encouraging the trend towards open and informal pre-trial meetings, and that the Law Society's system of certification be encouraged, although I appreciate there are certain difficulties in that.

The final recommendation reflects what has to be one of the underlying concerns about the whole debate, the question of medical accountability. The Working Party appears to accept this concern and proposes what might be regarded as complaints procedures separate from claims procedures. Whether or not this would lead to the medical profession being swamped with complaints is a matter for speculation. There is an argument that the present system insulates doctors from a lot of complaints, because the aggrieved patient takes legal advice on his or her problem, finds that there is no likelihood of bringing a successful case and the matter is simply allowed to drop. This might not be the case if compensation were collected as a matter of right, and the aggrieved patient could then pursue a complaint against the doctor, not involving substantial costs as far as the plaintiff is concerned but which may lead to considerable trouble and expense for the doctor. This opens up questions as to whether or not medical insurance would be available to enable a doctor to clear his or her name if a complaint were brought, even though the complaint would not lead to financial consequences that might currently be met by insurance cover. The Report does not explore these issues—it merely identifies the possibilities—but that could be quite an interesting debate in itself.

*Summary*

The Report's Summary repeats the Working Party's view that a limited no-fault scheme would be a means by which reasonable levels of compensation could be provided promptly to the victims of medical intervention at relatively low administrative cost and with fair ease of accessibility for those involved. This may be so, but the next sentence in the Report says it all: 'However, the scheme would need to be carefully costed before implementation'.

## Conclusion

The main purpose of this Report was to encourage public debate on the question of establishing first principles and then, depending upon the outcome of that debate, to move forward, backward or sideways, as the case may be—whichever way, it has to be better than the present system. My personal view is that the government's present initiative with regard to improving court procedures, and the attitude of those involved in the provision of legal services, will lead to a significant improvement, but that should not preclude further debate.


# APPENDIX

*Recommendations and Summary.* Reprinted from *Compensation for adverse consequences of medical intervention.*


## Recommendations

The Working Party became aware during the course of considering the various options for reform that there remained inequities in any no-fault scheme limited to medical interventions, which arise out of the inherent difficulties in determining causation in this area (see Chapter 2). It was felt that the only permanent solution to these difficulties would be the implementation of a comprehensive disability income scheme for all illness- and injury-related disability irrespective of causation. However, it was recognised that, by its very nature, such a solution would require a trade-off to be made between the generosity of compensation and the breadth of coverage. The cost of such a scheme would therefore depend upon how this trade-off was resolved through the political process. In the absence of any impending resolution of this issue, the Working Party wishes to make the following recommendations:

### *Introduction of a no-fault scheme*

1. *It is recommended that* a no-fault scheme, limited to compensating the adverse consequences of medical intervention, should be introduced with the following features:

    i Economic damages recoverable under such a scheme should be capped, and prospective loss of earnings should be limited to average net earnings.

    ii Non-economic damages (eg pain and suffering) should also be capped.

    iii Those wishing to avoid any shortfall in their expectations under such a scheme should have recourse to the insurance market and consideration should be given to making the premiums tax-deductible.

    iv Victims of medical mishaps should be disqualified from suing in negligence if they have already elected to claim under the no-fault compensation scheme on the same cause for action.

    v The amounts payable under the no-fault compensation scheme in the form of a lump sum should be strictly limited. Wherever practicable, periodic payments should be made, subject to review at stated intervals.

*Procedural rules for medical negligence actions*

**2.** For those actions which continue to be brought in medical negligence, *it is recommended that* procedural rules should be reviewed in the light of the following principles:

   **i** The court should be required to satisfy itself that evidence as to opinion (expert evidence) is admitted only from the medical witnesses of appropriate expertise. The Medical Royal Colleges and Faculties might give consideration to a way of ensuring that medical witnesses met this standard.

   **ii** The Working Party supports the view of the Master of Rolls that there should be the fullest disclosure of all material facts, and relevant opinions including medical reports. The judgement in the Naylor case made it clear that there should be only the strongest possible reason for refusing or failing to disclose material facts (*Naylor v. Preston AHA* [1987] 2 All ER 385).

   **iii** The Working Party welcomes the encouraging trend towards open and informal pre-trial meetings with a view to resolving matters in the interests of patients. We support the statement in the Civil Justice Review that there should be a greater exchange of reports between sides, as the oral aspect of pre-trial procedures can give rise to considerable delay (*Report of the Review Body on Civil Justice (1988)* Cm. 394 para. 76). We note the recent amendments to Order 38 of the Rules of the Supreme Court which permits the Court to direct the exchange of experts' reports (*Rules of the Supreme Court* (Amendment No. 4) 1989 (S.I. 1989 No. 2427)).

   **iv** The Working Party believes that the Law Society's system of certification of solicitors should be encouraged as a means of developing legal expertise in medical negligence.

*Medical accountability*

**3.** The Working Party accepts that one of the major criticisms of no-fault schemes has been that they might remove a source of medical accountability. *It is therefore recommended that* the scheme we have proposed above should be accompanied by a separate mechanism for the scrutiny of each claim in which doctors were involved to ensure that appropriate care had not been transgressed. If transgression is demonstrated, questions of professional discipline should be pursued. Movement towards this end might be achieved in the interim by the strengthening of medical audit and peer review, increased emphasis on the monitoring of medical performance, and the further development of risk management schemes operated by hospitals and health authorities. The Royal College itself has emphasised its commitment to this direction, by making the implementation of audit procedures a condition of recognition of training posts. As a hospital without training approval would find it difficult to obtain any junior staff, this represents a powerful incentive to implement such audit procedures, although the quality of the latter would need to be carefully monitored in future.

## National database

**4.** It is important that data on cases involving adverse consequences of medical intervention should be available for monitoring and scientific analysis. In the past the medical defence organisations have collected these data. The Working Party is concerned that health authorities should appreciate the importance of maintaining such a national database subsequent to the introduction of NHS Indemnity. *It is therefore recommended that* DHAs co-ordinate their approaches to this problem, either in conjunction with the defence organisations, or through the Department of Health. We believe that a comprehensive national database accessible to all would be an essential complement to the compensation reforms we have recommended above.

## Summary

We believe that a limited no-fault scheme along the lines we have proposed would be a means by which reasonable levels of compensation could be provided promptly to the victims of medical intervention at relatively low administrative cost and with relative accessibility for those involved. However, the scheme would need to be carefully costed before implementation. This means that detailed consideration be given to the likely effects on the numbers of people claiming compensation, and the levels of compensation payable, as well as the administrative costs involved. We recognise that the relatively low costs associated with the Swedish Patient Insurance Scheme follow from the generosity of the Swedish social security provision for the disabled in relation to economic loss. However, we believe that the restrictions we have suggested on the level of benefits under our proposed scheme are sufficient to imply an overall cost which is not excessive by comparison with the existing scheme, and that consideration should therefore be given to the appropriate means by which the scheme could be financed, and primary legislation drawn up. We should also emphasise that the improvements in the tort system, in accountability, and in data collection for risk management purposes are, in our view, essential adjuncts to any such compensation scheme. Indeed, they would appear to be desirable independently of any future implementation of our no-fault proposals.

## DISCUSSION

**Mr C. Hodges**: The recommendations at the end of the Report state that:

> The Working Party became aware during the course of considering the various options ... that there remained inequities in any no-fault scheme ... which arise out of the inherent difficulties in determining causation ... It was felt that the only permanent solution to these difficulties would be the implementation of a comprehensive disability income scheme for all illness- and injury-related disability irrespective of causation.

—but then say that they do not actually recommend it:

> by its very nature, such a solution would require a trade-off . . . between
> the generosity of compensation and the breadth of coverage. . . . In the
> absence of any impending resolution of this isssue, the Working Party
> . . . [recommends] . . . a no-fault scheme, . . .

This seems illogical and to fudge the issue, which is that they have
decided they would like to recommend a permanent disability scheme,
but know that it will not be possible—so they end up recommending a
no-fault scheme, also knowing that in the current political climate that
will not be possible either.

**Mr Milne**: Any realist today knows perfectly well that the present
government (or any immediate future government) would not fund the
so-called ideal solution and, even if it did, because of the number of
regulations, the sheer volume of paperwork that concerns our limited
social security system, it would not be a simple option. It may be fairer,
given the universality of payments to applicants, but will certainly not
start in the immediate future. I think the Report fairly describes certain
aspects of the present system and recognises the realism of the present
debate.

The problem is that the Working Party cannot put forward a positive
recommendation. I would have been happier if they had said, 'there are
funding problems, so how about simply concentrating on improving
the present system?'. The government could not take issue with
that—indeed, is moving towards it. This would then open up other
questions, such as access to justice because, at the same time as the
government is speeding up the courts, arguably fewer people are
getting access to the courts because of the legal aid restrictions.

**Mr R. Goldberg**: It is easy to talk about improving the present system,
but in this context it would be interesting to return to the case quoted by
Mr Milne, *Kay v. Ayrshire and Arran Health Board*, which concerned a
child with meningitis who was given huge overdoses of penicillin and
suffered severe deafness. The House of Lords eventually ruled that
where there are two competing causes, on the one hand penicillin and
on the other meningitis, it has to be shown that it is an accepted fact
that one of them is capable of causing or aggravating damage. It was
not shown in this case that penicillin was capable of causing or
aggravating deafness. There is no proof that penicillin can cause
deafness (there are very few cases where it may possibly be true), but it
is known that meningitis can cause deafness. What would the result of
this case be if the present system were improved? Perhaps we have to

start looking at it from the point of view of the needs of the patient as opposed to issues of causation.

**Mr Milne**: While I believe that the system can, should and will be improved, the underlying key issue is that such cases will always be potentially unfair because of the way the system works. The answer comes down to money; until the funding is available for such cases, there will be no real change.

**Mr Goldberg**: The Report said that a system of no-fault compensation could possibly be introduced irrespective of causation needing to be proved, but it suggests that it is important to establish a statistical data bank, to which doctors and pharmacists could provide information about the aetiology of cases. If there is no system of causation in a no-fault scheme, we will not be able to build up such a data bank.

**Dr D. Burley**: The tort system is possibly 'curable' but, if the College had thought that the shortcomings of the present tort system were likely to be cured in the next few years, it would not have set up a working party to prepare a report. We are worried about the quite considerable adverse consequences to patients of pending litigation. They may be in a litigation process for six or seven years; there is a tendency to perpetuate illness, to disrupt families, and also to create greed and avarice, as well as producing substantial and protracted anxiety on the part of doctors and disruption of their work. Then, of course, there is the practice of defensive medicine which has many disadvantages.

**Part 3**

---

# The European dimension

# Introduction to the European dimension

## Janice Webster
*Director General, Council of Bars and Law Societies of the European Community*

By now everyone is as familiar with the magic date '1992' as they were a few years ago with the George Orwell image of 1984. Just as 1984 came and went without any particular catastrophe, we can rest assured that 1992 will pass similarly—but by 31 December 1992 some 279 pieces of legislation should be in place to implement the plans for the integration of the internal market. In fact '1992' was simply a piece of clever PR by Lord Cockfield, who decided that it was necessary to set a target date to spur people into some activity and persuade them to achieve what ought to have been done many years ago.

The European Economic Community is all about achieving what are known as 'the four freedoms': the freedom of movement of capital, goods, persons and services. Following the founding Treaty there have been the single European Act, which has added the social dimension, including environmental law, and the developing jurisprudence of the European Court of Justice. European law now affects almost every aspect of our lives. It cannot be ignored, and as lawyers, pharmacists and doctors we cannot afford to ignore it if we value our professional insurance policies.

In 1974 Lord Denning said:

> 'The Treaty of Rome is like an incoming tide—it flows into the estuaries and back up the rivers. It cannot be held back. Parliament has decreed that the Treaty is henceforward to be part of our law. It is equal in force to any statute.'

In a later case in 1978 he went further, and said:

> 'It has not stopped at the high water mark. It has broken the dikes and the banks. It has submerged the surrounding land, so much so that we will have to learn to become amphibious if we wish to keep our heads above water.'

If that was true in 1978, it is certainly even more true now.

125

Doctors and lawyers are particularly involved in questions of free movement of persons, including mutual recognition of professional qualifications. In some ways, it is slightly easier for doctors, in that the human body is the same the world over, whereas both the legal systems and the spheres of activities of lawyers vary greatly. The medical profession has, however, had difficulties in defining what certain people, particularly the paramedicals, do in different countries and there have been a number of European Court of Justice cases in this regard. The main priority for the pharmaceutical industry is the free movement of goods.

At the end of January 1991 the Commission presented its proposals for the future system for the free movement of medicinal products for both human and veterinary use. These include:

— the establishment of a new European agency for the evaluation of medicinal products;
— the creation of a new centralised Community procedure, compulsory for biotechnology products and veterinary medicines used as performance enhancers, and optional for other innovatory medicinal products, leading to a Community authorisation valid throughout all 12 Member States;
— a decentralised procedure based on the principle of mutual recognition which will allow the progressive extension of a marketing authorisation from one Member State to the others, with important safeguards to ensure no dilution of the strict standards of quality, safety and efficacy.

The Commission has produced tables relating to the proposed decentralised and centralised procedures.

In addition, there is the draft Directive[1] on liability for defective services. This is a somewhat disturbing document, which has caused concern to some of those rendering professional services, in part because it reverses the burden of proof, and in part because of the definitions of 'services' and 'economic damage' contained therein, which some people consider extremely unsatisfactory.

In the following chapters acknowledged experts explain some of these matters. This will be of great interest and of practical value as we face the opportunities as well as the challenges of 1992.

## Reference

1. Proposal for a Directive of the Council of the European Community concerning the liability for defective services. COM(90) 482 final of 29/12/90—SYN 308.

# 10 | The European Community: its structure and relationship with the United Kingdom

## Euan F. Davidson

*Managing Partner, Wright, Johnston & Mackenzie, Solicitors, Glasgow*

---

## Introduction

The purpose of this chapter is to paint a picture of the organisation and structure of the European Communities, in particular their law-making role. In dealing with the relationship between the Communities and the UK I will confine myself to the nature and effect of Community law in a UK context.

When we talk about the European Community (EC) we are really talking about three Communities: the European Coal and Steel Community (ECSC), established in 1951; the European Economic Community (EEC), established by the Treaty of Rome in 1957; and the European Atomic Energy Community (Euratom), also established in 1957. At the time of establishment, all three European Communities had the same six participating members: France, Germany, Italy, Belgium, The Netherlands and Luxembourg. Both ECSC and Euratom have the simple aim of integrating specific sections of the economies of the Member States, coal and steel in the case of ECSC, and utilisation of atomic energy in the case of Euratom. It is the Economic Community, or Common Market, which deals with the establishment of the four fundamental freedoms: free movement of persons, services, goods and capital.

Originally the three communities had their own institutions, but since 1967, despite some differing terminology, they have effectively had one common set of institutions. It is rather like having a group of three companies with directors common to all. In law, there are three entities; in reality, there is arguably only one.

## Sovereignty

A glance at the popular press makes it clear that the EC is still seen by many in Britain as some kind of 'outsider'. Politicians have firmly

127

nailed the Union Jack to the mast and pledged to defend the concept of British sovereignty to the last drop. While this may be the British view, it is by no means a view shared by all other Community members. Indeed, it is probably fair to say that the attitudes of each Member State to Community membership and to the nature of the Community itself differ widely. While the question of UK sovereignty may be good matter for political rhetoric, the fact is that, by its accession to the EC Treaties, Britain has surrendered a substantial part of its sovereignty. The EC is a truly supranational body, although it is not easy to define its status. It resembles a state in that it is directed by political will and because it has created a new legal order. In terms of the Treaties, it has legal personality and the capacity to enter into diplomatic relations. Its institutions, however, cannot increase their power by their own decisions. To do so, they would require to go outside to the various Member States.

Member States have surrendered part of their sovereign rights in consideration for rights of participation in the Community and have become part of an international entity with its own authority and with a legal order independent of that of the individual Member States, to which Member States and all their citizens are subject.

## Supremacy of EC law

In the course of his long and distinguished career Lord Denning made a number of pronouncements on the subject of EC law. Perhaps one of the less colourful, but no less enlightening, of these was made in 1981 when he commented that

> Community law is now part of our law; and whenever there is any inconsistency, Community law has priority. It is not supplanting English law. It is part of our law which overrides any other part which is inconsistent with it. . . .

I submit that this statement is a correct representation of the position. The reference to English law could be replaced by a reference to Scots, French or Italian law or any other legal system having the force of law in any Member State. It is no longer enough for the lawyer to be acquainted with the provisions of UK statute and case law, but he must also be aware of what is happening in Brussels. While it is probably true that an increasing part of current UK statute law originates from Brussels' pronouncements, there are also EC rules applicable within this and every other Community country which have never been the subject of enactment by the national legislature. As progress continues towards 1992, almost every field of business is touched by the Community's legislative finger. Any lawyer who is not alive to the influence of EC law should look forward to a healthy increase in his professional indemnity premium in the future. To say that EC law has supremacy does not mean that its rules are better than national laws, but that it takes precedence over them, whether that national legislation is made before or after the relevant Community provision. In the face of contrary Community law, national law must give way.

The primary sources of EC law are the Treaties that established ECSC, Euratom and the EEC. By signing the Treaties (or the accession Treaties thereto) Member States have given up certain sovereign rights to the institutions of the Community. The fundamental principles of EC membership and the constitution of the EC institutions are all dealt with within the framework of the Treaties.

The secondary legislation of the EC is likely to be far more relevant in day-to-day practice. In terms of Article 189 of the EEC Treaty, the Council and the Commission have the power to make Regulations, issue Directives, take decisions, make recommendations and deliver opinions. Regulations and Directives are of particular importance.

*Regulations* are directly applicable within every Member State and are binding in their entirety. No further action is needed by the Member State to give them force. They can be issued by either the Council of Ministers or the European Commission (the latter under delegated authority). Individual states have no choice as to whether or not to implement a Regulation and no flexibility about the means of implementation or the wording to be used. The Regulation is issued by the Council or Commission, and from the moment it comes into force it is as effective in the United Kingdom as if it were an Act of Parliament. Regulations tend to be reasonably detailed so as to be capable of enforcement. They are used frequently in relation to the Common Agricultural Policy (CAP) and also in matters of competition law.

*Directives* are slightly different. These are pronouncements of the Council addressed to each Member State, setting out defined objectives to be achieved usually by legislation by each Member State. The choice of method of implementation and the exact wording is left to the state in question, which must take the necessary steps to bring the provisions of the Directive into force within the timetable laid down in the Directive. In other words, Directives are binding as to the result to be achieved, and each Member State decides how to amend or extend its existing legislation to achieve this. Many Directives, therefore, simply set out broad issues of principle and leave the rest to the national government, whereas others look more like Regulations; for example, in Council Directive 86/457 on specific training for general medical practice, not much discretion is left to national legislation.

It would not be safe to ignore Directives as a source of EC law on the basis that unless they have been passed into law within the UK they have no effect. It is not quite so simple. The Courts will give effect to Directives which should, according to their terms, have been adopted by the national legislature even where the legislature has failed to do this. In the context of today's discussions, Directives are probably more relevant than Regulations, and it is vital not only for the academic but also for the practitioner to be aware of their precise terms.

Regulations and Directives have one further difference. Regulations are cited with the number of the Regulation first and the year at the end, whereas Directives are cited the other way round. Thus, 87/22 is a Directive, and 4087/88 a Regulation.

## The institutions of the EC

For a description, in layman's terms, of how the institutions of the Community function I can recommend *Working Together* (2nd edition, 1988), by Emile Noel, a former Secretary General of the Commission, published by the Commission of the EC. Broadly speaking, there are four EC institutions:

— the Commission
— the Council of Ministers
— the Parliament
— the Courts

### The Commission

The European Commission is the institution which we in Britain often find the most difficult to understand. It is often referred to as the Community's civil service, and is probably the target of most of the jibes concerning Eurocrats. In fact, it is rather more than a civil service, and its bureaucracy is not as big as might be imagined. At present, the Commission consists of 17 Commissioners and staff of about 10,000 (which compares favourably with any local council). The Commission has a leading role to play in the legislative process, in that it proposes, executes and enforces the policies of the Community. Commissioners are required to be nationals of Member States, but during their time on the Commission they owe no allegiance to their Member State. In terms of the Treaties, their independence must be guaranteed and they can neither seek nor take instructions from any national government or body. The larger Member States (France, Germany, Spain, Italy and the UK) each appoint two Commissioners, and the smaller states one

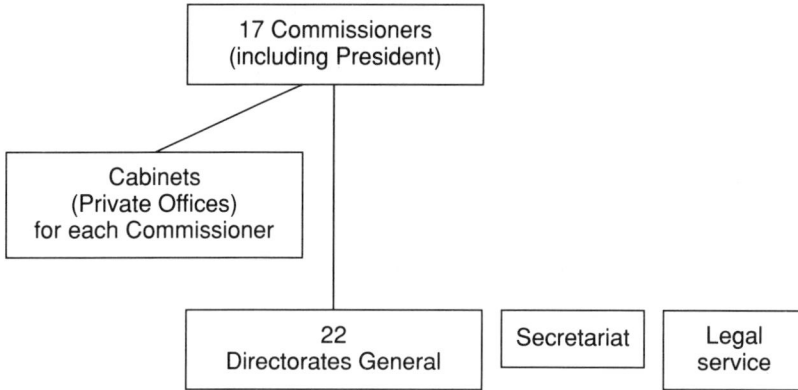

**Fig. 1.** Organisation of the Commission.

each. The British Commissioners traditionally are appointed one from each of the larger political parties.

Each commissioner is responsible for a number of directorates general, of which there are 22 at present. In the present context, the most relevant will probably be DGIII (internal markets and industrial affairs), DGIV (competition), DGVI (veterinary medicine), and DGXII (science, research and development). Each directorate general is usually but not always responsible to one commissioner, and is headed by a director general who will generally be a specialist in his own field and of a different nationality from the commissioner whom he serves. In addition, each commissioner is served by a chef de cabinet who is the head of the commissioner's own private office.

In addition to the directorates general and each commissioner's cabinet, the Commission civil service is completed by a secretariat general (headed by the Secretary General who is the most senior member of Commission staff) and a number of special bodies such as Legal Services and the Statistical Office. Broadly speaking, the Commission has four major roles:

1. *Initiation of policy.* Following up ideas from many sources (including the commissioners themselves), the Commission takes a major role in shaping the measures to be adopted by the Council of Ministers. The Council can do nothing without a proposal from the Commission. Many hundreds of proposals are put up each year.
2. *Legislative and executive.* Under all the Treaties, the Commission is given authority to ensure that Treaty provisions are carried out. It can also receive delegated powers from the Council of Ministers. The Commission therefore can itself issue Regulations, and indeed

the number of Regulations made in a single year by the Commission may run into four figures (mostly relating to the CAP). The Commission ensures that the rules of the Treaties are applied to particular cases.

3. *Representative and administrative.* The Commission represents the Community in diplomatic matters and administers many of the funds within the Community's budget.

4. *Watchdog.* The Commission acts as a watchdog, ensuring that Treaty obligations are observed. If there is an allegation of breach of these obligations, it is for the Commission to investigate it, reach a conclusion and notify the action necessary to correct the error. In effect, it is policeman, judge and jury. It recently gave a reasoned opinion to the UK government in respect of the latter's alleged failure to implement correctly the Product Liability Directive. If a Member State who has defaulted does not comply with the Commission's opinion it will be brought before the Court of Justice.

## The Council of Ministers

The Council of Ministers is the supreme authority and the decision making body of the Community. It consists of representatives of the Member States, with each government delegating to it one of its members, who sit not as individuals but as representatives of their country (unlike the Commission whose members are independent). Meetings take place between Ministers themselves. A separate body, however, the Committee of Permanent Representatives (COREPER) prepares the work of the Council and carries out its mandates. Presidency of the Council rotates on a six-monthly basis.

Under the Treaties, the Council has powers of decision making which are legally binding throughout the Community. Subject to minor exceptions, the Council may act only on a proposal put to it by the Commission. It is open for the Council to invite a proposal from the Commission, but without a proposal it cannot take a decision. Unanimity or a qualified majority (54 out of the usual 76 votes) is generally required before a proposal can become law. Each Member State has a set number of votes, with the four larger countries (France, Germany, Italy and the UK) each having ten votes, Spain eight, Belgium, Greece, the Netherlands and Portugal five, Denmark and Ireland three, and Luxembourg two. Rights of veto exist in certain circumstances.

## The Parliament

The role of the Parliament (or Assembly) in the EC is to bring a democratic element into the workings of the Community. The Parliament meets in Strasbourg, although its committees usually sit in Brussels and the secretariat (to complicate matters) meets in Luxembourg. An Assembly has always existed, but it was not until 1979 that it was an elected body. It is ill-advised, however, to view the European Parliament as being similar to the UK Parliament. In terms of the Treaties, it exercises only advisory and supervisory powers, although in practice certain budgetary powers are also available to it. The participation of the EC Parliament in the legislative process is extremely limited, although it must be consulted, and it has itself resolved to exploit to the limit the opportunities available to play a greater role therein. Another function of the Parliament is to ask questions of, and obtain answers from, the Council and the Commission, and in extreme cases it can adopt a motion of censure and force the Commission to resign *en bloc*, but does not have the power to remove individual Commissioners.

## The Courts

The fourth institution is the Courts. There is a Court of Auditors, and now also a Court of First Instance. I will however concentrate on the European Court of Justice, based in Luxembourg, which must not be confused with the International Court in The Hague or the European Court of Human Rights in Strasbourg. The Court of Justice has a substantial role to play in dealing with cases brought by the Commission against national governments for infringement of the Treaties. Similarly, governments may bring actions against the Commission in relation to its decisions. The Court has increasingly been called upon to give preliminary rulings on questions of Community law referred to it by national courts. In the first 20-odd years of the EC's existence, the Court heard about 3,000 actions in relation to the Treaty of Rome, about half of which were preliminary rulings, about 500 actions taken by the Commission, 119 by governments and just over 600 by individuals.

## The legislative process

Stated briefly, the legislative process takes the following route:
1. A proposal is prepared for the Commission. Experts are consulted, usually being appointed by national governments at the request of the Commission.
2. The Commission decides on a proposal, which is then submitted to the Council of Ministers.
3. The Council sends the proposal to the European Parliament and

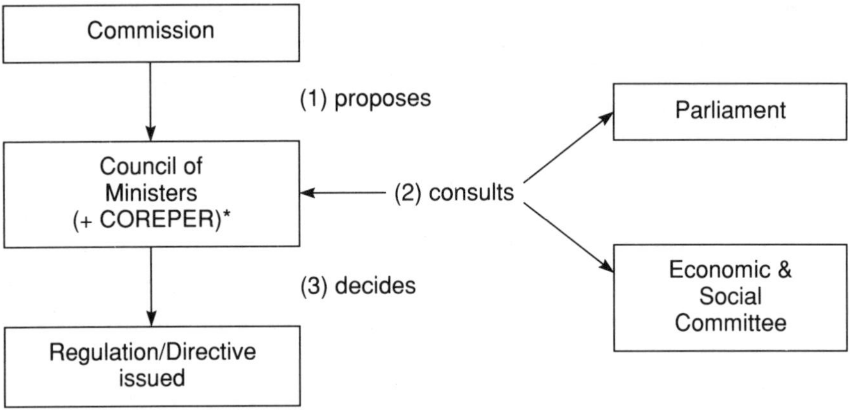

* COREPER = Committee of Permanent Representatives

**Fig. 2.** The legislative process, EC dimension, on non-single market matters.

also to the Economic and Social Committee (a consultative body made up of representatives of employers, workers and other business interests throughout the Community) who discuss the matter with the Commission.

4. The Council takes a decision, based on the Commission's proposal and the opinions received from the Parliament and the Economic and Social Committee. This discussion usually takes place within COREPER.

5. Assuming agreement has been reached by COREPER, the matter is referred to the Council and rubber-stamped. If there is no agreement in COREPER, the Council discusses the matter in an attempt to arrive at a consensus.

6. Certain single market legislation requires a greater involvement of the European Parliament in the procedure. In these cases (which relate to harmonisation measures and the four freedoms), the Council does not make a final decision on a Commission proposal but instead adopts a 'common position' by a qualified majority of 54 of the 76 votes. This common position is then referred to Parliament, and within three months Parliament can approve, amend, reject or effectively ignore it. If approved or ignored, the Council proceeds to final decision. If rejected, it may proceed to a final decision only on a unanimous vote. If amended, the Commission is given one month to carry out the amendment before re-submission to the Council. On re-submission, Council may adopt the Commission's revised proposal by a qualified majority. If it wishes to adopt parliamentary

amendments which the Commission has not included or itself to
amend the Commission's proposal, it must do so on a unanimous
basis. Alternatively, it may fail to act, and if it has not acted within
three months the Commission proposal will lapse. The purpose of
these new rules on single market legislation is to give the European
Parliament greater power—but the Council still has the last word.

## The enforcement of EC law

While EC law may emanate from Brussels this does not mean that it
can be enforced only before the European Courts in Luxembourg. EC
law is now part of the UK legal system. If formally incorporated within
the law of the UK by a positive Act, for example, a Directive taking
shape as an Act of Parliament, enforcement will, by definition, be
through the UK courts. Directives which are 'time expired' (as discussed above) and Regulations may also be enforced directly before the
UK courts. Difficulties of interpretation can be referred to the European Court for a decision. In this way, EC law can be enforced by the
courts as easily as 'indigenous' matters of national law. In areas of
greater or wider policy, the Commission can (as previously discussed)
initiate proceedings before the European Court of Justice, as may
national governments or individuals aggrieved by a Commission decision. Substantial fines may be imposed for breaches of the Treaties,
particularly in competition law matters.

Nobody should be in any doubt as to the enforceability of the
Community legal order. It is as relevant to present or future decisions
on matters of business or research as UK law. Indeed, in some areas, it
may be more relevant than UK law due to the content of the Commission's programme. We ignore it at our peril.

# 11 | The European Community interest in pharmaceuticals

**Noreen Burrows**

*Professor of European Law, University of Glasgow*

## Introduction

The aim of this chapter is to explain the European Community's interest in pharmaceutical medicine. I hope to provide the background which explains why Community law has been, and is being, developed in relation to pharmaceutical medicine. My aim is not, therefore, to outline all the areas of law concerned. I see my remit as providing a framework for discussion of these substantive areas of law.

To explain the European Community's interest in pharmaceutical medicine, I have to begin with the cumbersome statement that the Community is based on a customs union whereby, in addition to legal rules on tariffs, quantitative restrictions and measures of equivalent effect to tariffs and quantitative restrictions, the founding treaties of the European Communities provide for the free movement of goods, persons, services and capital. To make the issues more palatable for those who are not fascinated by Community law I will set up a number of scenarios (or case studies) to present the issues in a less legalistic way.

## Scenarios

### 1. *The rejected practitioner*

Imagine the case of a young, bright and enthusiastic medical practitioner, a member of the Faculty of Pharmaceutical Medicine, fluent in several European languages, who sees a plum job advertised in any country of the European Community which is not his or her own. Our practitioner applies for the post, and is rejected on the grounds that he or she is British and/or that his or her qualifications are not recognised in that state.

## 2.  *The rejected product*

A large and respected pharmaceutical company develops a new drug for the relief of pain. The drug has been clinically tested and approved by the licensing authority of the Member State concerned. It is a drug which is widely used in the home state, and the company has willing buyers in state X, but the authorities in the latter state consider the drug to be unsafe and prohibit its importation.

## 3.  *The frustrated whizz-kids*

The case of the frustrated whizz-kids centres on the development of a new medical product by bringing together two existing products. The whizz-kids in company A produce a drug which relieves a certain medical condition but has unpleasant side-effects. The whizz-kids in company B produce the drug which limits the side-effects. A and B wish to get together for the purposes of research, marketing and licensing the drug.

## 4.  *The protective state*

The protective state produces a list of drugs which may be prescribed by the health service of that state. Oddly enough, omitted from the list are a number of products, produced and distributed in other Member States of the European Communities and in free circulation there.

These four scenarios are over-simplified but can be used to illustrate the fact that the European Community must be involved in developing legal rules governing all aspects of the practice of pharmaceutical medicine if the aims of the Community are to be fulfilled: that individuals may move freely within the Community to live and work, and that products developed and sold in one Member State can be exported without hindrance. Of course, freeing the market in this way could make for a law of the jungle, so European law must maintain standards of quality, protect consumers and patients, and ensure that any new European rules are effectively enforced. Anyone involved with pharmaceutical medicine will, therefore, be immediately affected by European law in most aspects of his or her work.

## The legal rules

Community law is contained in the treaties (especially the EEC Treaty and the Single European Act) and in legislation adopted by way of Regulations or Directives by the Community institutions. Regulations become law immediately and do not normally require legislation on the part of the Member States. Directives, whether or not they create direct effects, must be implemented by national legislation. In the UK, Directives are normally implemented either by adoption of new Acts of Parliament or by amendment to existing legislation. Alternatively, the European Communities Act 1972 (an Act of the UK Parliament) gives ministers the powers to adopt delegated legislation where necessary. These instruments must be laid before Parliament in accordance with our own constitutional practices. Such changes to our laws can include changes to both substantive and procedural rules.

It should be pointed out that, despite the current obsession with the date of 31 December 1992, the basis for Community action is essentially in the provisions of the EEC Treaty; 1992 is merely a date set for the adoption by the Community institutions of a legislative programme which completes the task set out in the EEC Treaty.

## The free movement of persons

The EEC Treaty foresees an area in which there will be complete mobility of labour. It sets out certain rights, for example, the right to take up employment in another Member State of the Community, which are secured for all nationals of the other Member States. In practice, the rights of free movement are not so simple, and the Community has had to adopt further legislation to guarantee the operation of the rules.

Scenario 1 shows some of the hurdles which national law imposes; for example, the requirement that some jobs must have nationally approved qualifications would be an almost complete barrier to someone wishing to take up employment elsewhere other than in his or her Member State. The Community solution has been to harmonise professional qualifications, by recognising the qualifications gained in one State as being equivalent to those gained in another. Specific Directives have been adopted for medical practitioners. Other professionals, such as lawyers, are covered by a general Directive on mutual recognition. In this way, our rejected practitioner can use Community law to challenge national legal restrictions.

## The free movement of goods

Community law demands that goods which are lawfully produced and marketed in one Member State of the Community should be free to be exported to the other 11 Member States. This presents no major problem with cricket bats, but in the case of production and marketing of drugs, however, all Member States demand that these products must be safe and effective in order to protect their own citizens. Such national measures could completely thwart the creation of a single market in pharmaceutical products. The Member States and the Community institutions recognise the need to adopt a balance between the creation of an open market and the health and safety of their citizens. The Community response has been to take action on several different fronts:

1.  The adoption of Community-wide standards of product liability.
2.  The development of Community-wide regulatory regimes.
3.  The limitation of the effects of national rules on pricing of goods, to avoid the possibility that Member States can use pricing policies as a barrier to the free movement of goods.
4.  The adoption of Community law on the presentation of medicinal products, including labelling and packaging.

In these three areas Community law has either been, or is in the process of being, adopted to balance the genuine and legitimate concerns relating to drug safety and use against the desire to create an open market. In scenario 2, therefore, Community law should aid the companies concerned to export their products but, at the same time, safeguard the interests of the importing state as it seeks to protect its own citizens.

## Competition law

The competition law of the Community attempts to ensure that the national barriers being broken down to create a common market are not rebuilt by the companies themselves. Competition law, therefore, places an obligation on private and public undertakings not to pursue restrictive business practice or to abuse their market power in ways which affect trade between Member States. Certain agreements between undertakings are, therefore, prohibited. These rules effectively limit the options of companies in pursuing joint production, marketing and licensing or research and development. However, Community law also recognises the adverse consequences which a strict application of competition rules might place on companies in terms of innovation and consequent benefits to consumers.

Community law has, therefore, been developed by the adoption of Regulations and also by decisions of the Commission and the European Court of Justice, setting out the limits under which joint research, licensing and marketing are permissible. The potentially collusive behaviour of our whizz-kids in scenario 3 is therefore governed by the competition rules of the Community. In addition, Community law is developing rapidly in the area of intellectual property law, to provide a Community framework for patents and other forms of intellectual property, for example, in the field of biotechnology.

## Public procurement

Scenario 4 is a grossly over-simplified view of the role of the state in protecting national interests. Such protection comes not only from direct discrimination against non-national products but also from the selective use of pricing policies and control, selective aid to research, and procedures which tend to favour local interests. In this respect, the Community has adopted a discrete approach—the Community can almost be said to have respected these national policies. However, attempts are being made to open up national procurement markets, with the adoption of legislation on pricing, transparency of aid and public procurement. The provision of computing facilities by health boards, to take one example, is subject to Community procurement rules.

Depending upon the point of view, these developments in Community law can be seen from different perspectives. From the point of view of a Community law practitioner, they are a welcome, interesting and financially rewarding area of legal activity. From the Community's point of view, Community action seeks to reduce 'the costs of non-Europe'. This inelegant phrase sums up the Commission's attempts to create a fully functioning single market which reduces the inefficiencies of our present nationally divided economies. In the pharmaceuticals sector, the Cecchini[1] Report on the benefits of the single market sums up this view as follows:

> By and large, the research tends to support the view that Community legislation aimed at further freeing of the European pharmaceuticals market could release considerable resources. These could be used to increase company margins, thus improving the capacity of firms to innovate, and to reduce drug prices, thus reducing public expenditure.

## Conclusions

It is indisputable that there are inefficiencies in the pharmaceutical market. It is, however, debatable whether the methods chosen by the Commission to reduce such inefficiencies will be effective. Individual pieces of Community legislation have caused both concern and debate within Member States, one major concern being that the removal of alleged inefficiencies might result in a loss of existing safeguards to the detriment of consumers as a whole. In this respect, I would not be a true academic if I were not to say that more research is necessary in order to evaluate these claims.

Finally, I can only hazard a guess as to what view a member of the Faculty of Pharmaceutical Medicine will take of these legal developments. Evidence presented to the House of Lords Select Committee on the European Communities in 1990 to assist in their evaluation of the Commission's proposals on the distribution, supply and labelling of medicinal products suggests that there is not an industry-wide viewpoint.[2] There is scope, however, for this Faculty to put forward its views to bodies such as the House of Lords Select Committee and the European Commission and Parliament. It could play an active role in helping to develop European-wide legislation in this area of pharmaceutical law which is in a very interesting stage of its evolution.

### References

1. Cecchini, P. (1988). *1992 The European Challenge*: Gower Press, Aldershot, p. 68.
2. House of Lords Select Committee on the European Communities, Session 1989–90, 20th Report, HL Paper 77.

# 12 | Parallel imports and EC law

**Leigh Hancher**

*Professor of Public Economic Law, Erasmus University, Rotterdam,*
*The Netherlands*

## Introduction

The phenomenon of parallel imports in the European Community (EC) is largely the result of the considerable price differences between the various national markets. In particular, major differences exist between the southern European countries, where national governments impose strict price controls, and the northern Member States, where price control is either non-existent (Germany) or more lenient (UK). Price divergences may be as much as 500 per cent between the highest and lowest price countries within the Community.[1] The patents on numerous 'market leaders' have either expired in recent years or will do so within the next decade. Patent protection, together with trade mark protection for brand names, is essential to the process of product differentiation within the pharmaceutical market, which in turn enables manufacturers to enjoy a dominant position on the market for particular therapies. There is usually very little price competition between products on specific therapeutic submarkets, although this is gradually changing within the Community. On the one hand, when a product's patent lapses, there may emerge *interbrand* competition (that is, competition between the original product and products marketed by competing manufacturers under a different brand name or under a non-branded generic name). Free movement of patented, branded pharmaceuticals, on the other hand, may eventually lead to an increase in *intrabrand* competition in the Community.

Unfortunately, however, complete free movement of pharmaceutical products is not yet a reality in the EC, even if the creation of a common European market for pharmaceutical products has been a long-standing Community objective. In its '*White Book*', of 1985, the Commission laid down a timetable for the elimination of a series of obstacles to pharmaceutical trade.[2] Of particular importance to the future feasibility of parallel trade are the Commission's plans to suppress the requirement that every new medicine must obtain a marketing authorisation at national level. National product licensing requirements, together with industrial property right protection, have undoubtedly been one of the main contributors to the continued compartmentalisation of the Community market. This in turn allows manufacturers to charge different prices in different markets.

The future feasibility of parallel trading in pharmaceuticals in the EC will therefore depend upon the interaction of progress towards harmonisation on two fronts. On the one hand, if national price controls and *reimbursement* controls are more closely aligned, there will be fewer incentives for pharmacists and retailers to purchase parallel imported products. On the other hand, the harmonisation of product licensing controls will facilitate trade in all types of product, including parallel products. Much depends, however, upon the methods chosen to harmonise product licensing and the selection of the types of products which are to benefit from harmonised procedures. Finally, even if there is progress towards harmonisation of safety licensing criteria, the continued importance of industrial property rights as a potential means of protecting original products against competition from parallel imports cannot be ignored.

This chapter examines each of these issues in turn. First, the Commission's attempts to align price and reimbursement controls, discussing in this context the important ruling of the Court of Justice in Case 249/88 *Commission v. Belgium*. Secondly, the latest Commission proposals on harmonising safety legislation and their implications for parallel products. It is evident from the latest set of proposals that established older products will probably not benefit from the new centralised procedures, but will continue to be subject to national licensing procedures. In this section, I shall examine the case law on mutual recognition of national licensing procedures, with particular reference to the most recent decision of the Court of Justice, Case 347/89 *Freistaat Bayern v. Eurim-Pharm*. Thirdly, the growing importance of industrial property protection and, in particular, the latest proposals for the new supplementary protection certificate are considered.

## Pricing and reimbursement

It is well-known that the Community institutions have relatively restricted powers to prevent Member States from adopting various types of price or profit control measures or from drawing up various types of 'limited' or 'selective' lists, unless these types of measures are in conflict with Article 30 of the Treaty, which prohibits quantitative restrictions on imports or measures having an equivalent effect. It is

equally well-known that national law does not have to be discrimina-
tory to fall foul of Article 30.

The Court applied its general principles for the first time to price
controls within the drug sector in Case 181/82 *Roussel*. It reiterated its
established case law on price measures to the effect that:

> ... although such systems do not in themselves constitute measures
> having an effect equivalent to a quantitative restriction, they may have
> such an effect when the prices are fixed at a level such that the sale of
> imported products becomes either impossible or more difficult than that
> of domestic products.

As for maximum profit controls, the Court has held that these rules
do not infringe Community law provided that the producers remain
free to determine their own retail prices, and could thereby adapt their
prices to their own cost structures (Case 78/82 *Commission v. Italy*; Case
231/83 *Cullet*; and most recently, Case 249/88 *Commission v. Belgium*).

The application of this principle to the pharmaceutical sector has
caused a number of problems. In two recent cases the Court has held
that systems of calculating prices which allowed manufacturers to
include the major part of their costs incurred in a particular Member
State, but which did not make sufficient allowance for costs incurred in
importation, infringed Article 30. In both cases, however, the Commission had not provided sufficient substantive evidence of discrimination against imports (Case 56/87 *Commission v. Italy*; Case 249/88
*Commission v. Belgium*).

The Court has also upheld the legality of reimbursement schemes. In
Case 238/82 *Duphar* it considered the legality of a negative list, and
held that such schemes are compatible with Article 30 where the
schemes were compiled on an objective and verifiable basis.

The Commission drew on this case law to compile a *Communication
on prices*, published in 1986, which purported to state the various
obligations of the Member States under existing Community Law
(O.J. 1986 C310/7). In 1989, the Council adopted a Directive relating
to the transparency of measures regulating the pricing of medicinal
products for human use and their inclusion in the scope of national
health insurance schemes (no. 89/105 O.J. 1988). The purpose of this
measure is to commence a process whereby disparities in price and
reimbursement regulatory schemes are gradually eliminated. The
measure is very much a first step—it merely requires a certain amount
of transparency in the way in which pricing and related decisions are
taken. Its Article 9 provides that the Commission will make a new
proposal to the Council by December 1991. The Commission is due to
publish a position paper on this matter shortly. It must be acknowledged that it has received a significant setback from the Court's ruling

in Case 249/88 *Commission v. Belgium*, which *inter alia* considered the concept of transparency.

Case 249/88 concerned an enforcement action brought against the Belgian government by the Commission. The latter contended that the Belgian government had breached Article 30 on three counts:

1. The system of maximum price controls.
2. The reimbursement regime.
3. The imposition of various contractual agreements with the pharmaceutical industry.

The Commission failed to substantiate its claims under (1) and (2). In the course of the proceedings, the Commission had also alleged that the Belgian government had failed to comply with the principles of objectivity and transparency in decision making, as required by Directive 89/105. This argument found favour with Advocate General Tesauro, who argued that the criteria on which all pricing and reimbursement decisions were taken should be 'reasoned' and made available to the applicant. Failure to guarantee a sufficient degree of transparency resulted in a breach of Article 30. Unfortunately, the Court did not follow its Advocate General.

As far as decisions on prices are concerned, the Court held that the Commission had not substantiated its claim that the minister had *refused* to provide reasoned decisions on individual prices. For reimbursement, it sufficed that the individual companies had the possibility of entering a 'dialogue' with the competent authorities on decisions to include or exclude their products from reimbursement lists. It might be suggested, with respect, that the aim of the principle of transparency is to allow potential competitors, as well as the individual firms concerned, to assess the reasonableness of the decisions in question.

Given this conservative interpretation of the transparency concept, it is evident that progress even towards the first stage of harmonising price control will be very slow. Hence continued scope for pharmaceutical price regulation remains at Community level. It is of course important to bear in mind that national reimbursement rules are becoming increasingly finely-tuned, and Member States are devising ways of recouping some of the profits which pharmacists may make from substituting parallel imports for the more costly original.

## Harmonisation of safety legislation

Despite the fact that the Community began the task of harmonising pharmaceutical legislation as long ago as 1965, it has not yet realised its stated aim of eliminating the need for separate national licences in every Member State. In 1983, the Commission set a deadline of 1990 for the realisation of the automatic mutual recognition of national drug marketing authorisations or licences throughout the Community.[3] In late 1990, it produced a package of draft Regulations and Directives setting out the means to achieve this goal (see Chapter 13). If these proposals are approved, after 1992 there will be three distinct authorisation procedures:

1. A centralised Community procedure, reserved for certain new medicinal products and valid for all 12 Member States.
2. A decentralised procedure which will cover a substantial majority of medicinal products, based upon the principle of mutual recognition.
3. National procedures limited in principle to applications concerning a single Member State.

Use of the centralised procedure will be compulsory for medicinal products derived from biotechnology, and will be available on an optional basis for other high-technology medicinal products and new chemical entities. Applications for authorisation will be submitted directly to a European Medicines Agency, consisting primarily of a reinforced Committee for Proprietary Medicinal Products (CPMP) and supported by an administrative and technical secretariat.

The objective of the decentralised procedure is to permit the extension of a marketing authorisation granted in one Member State to one or more of the others by recognising the original authorisation. In the case of serious objections, and after examining all possibilities for a bilateral resolution of the problem, the CPMP will arbitrate.

In this case, common to the parallel pharmaceutical products market,where the original products are already licensed both on the market of origin and on that of destination, will the parallel importer still be obliged to obtain a licence?[4] The case law on Article 30 of the EEC Treaty, prohibiting measures having effects equivalent to quantitative restrictions on trade, suggests that its terms might already *imply* the concepts of mutual recognition and mutual acceptance. It is of course well-known that national rules on marketing authorisations may fall foul of the Treaty's provisions on the free movement of goods,[5] but the European Court has generally been cautious about requiring mutual recognition where issues of public health are involved, particularly where there are substantial national variations in the appraisal of scientific test data.

In its decision in Case 104/75 *De Peijper*,[6] concerning the importation of Valium into the Netherlands by an independent importer, the drug had been duly licensed by its original manufacturer and therefore lawfully marketed in both countries. For importation, however, Dutch legislation required the presentation of certain documentation verified by the manufacturer. Centrafarm, the importer, argued that as it could not obtain the co-operation of Hoffmann-La Roche to present this documentation, it was prevented from importing Valium into the Netherlands. The Court ruled that national practices which had the effect of channelling trade in such a way that only certain firms could effect these imports constituted a measure having an effect equivalent to a quantitative restriction. Although it recognised that Member States were entitled under Article 36 to enact measures protecting public health, such measures were limited to those which were necessary to achieve that objective. In this instance, the product in question had been licensed in both countries, and was, furthermore, similar in every respect to the product which had been imported through the manufacturer's authorised channels. In the Court's view, there were alternative ways of protecting public health, including active co-operation between the national authorities or between the latter and the original licence holder.

It is therefore clear from the judgment that, in the absence of harmonising measures, product licensing regimes were not in themselves contrary to Article 30 but could be permitted under Article 36 as long as their operation was in line with Treaty objectives. It must be emphasised, first, that *De Peijper* concerned an imported product which was *therapeutically equivalent* to the domestic product, and secondly, that the Court interpreted Articles 30 and 36 to require only less onerous administrative procedures for the licensing for such products, and not automatic mutual acceptance of a product licensed elsewhere in the Community.[7]

In its later case law on the scope of public health exception, either under Article 36 or as one of the recognised mandatory requirements justifying restrictions to trade resulting from national measures which are equally applicable to domestic and imported products,[8] the Court has applied the twin principles of proportionality and the prohibition against arbitrary discrimination to eliminate a variety of national administrative requirements. It has exercised more caution, however, in cases involving claims of equivalence, or mutual acceptance of complex scientific testing requirements, and has frequently left the determination of equivalence to the national courts. The greater the scientific uncertainty surrounding the methodology employed or the results rendered, the more willing the Court has been to allow Member States to adopt different approaches. This cautious approach is also reflected in its more recent case law on the importation of 'borderline' products, and on the extent to which pharmacists can continue to enjoy a monopoly over the distribution of certain types of 'medicinal' products in individual Member States. Given that there is only a partial degree of harmonisation at Community level, the Court has been prepared to allow Member States to continue to rely on Article 36, providing that the relevant national rules do not result in discrimination against imported products.[9]

Thus, the Court has condemned national rules on pharmaceutical product safety which require that the person responsible for placing the goods on the market should be resident in that country,[10] and a requirement that enterprises supplying domestic retail chemists directly must maintain premises locally.[11] In a recent case involving the importation of medicinal products for personal use, the Court ruled that the purchase of a medicinal product in a pharmacy of another Member State gives a guarantee equivalent to that resulting from the sale of the medicinal product by a pharmacy in the Member State where it is imported, especially because conditions of entry into the pharmacy profession are subject to harmonising Directives.[12] This concept of an equivalent level of protection had been developed by the Court's ruling in the earlier Case 272/80 *Biologische producten*[13] that where the results of the various chemical analyses were available to the importing authorities, they were not unnecessarily to insist on duplicative testing.[14] Member States have a duty to assist in bringing about a relaxation of the controls existing in intra-Community trade.

This line of case law has recently been considered by the Court of Justice in Case 347/89 *Freistaat Bayern v. Eurim-Pharm GmbH*. Eurim-Pharm attempted to import into Germany certain products legally marketed in other Member States. Under German law, it is necessary *inter alia* to obtain a customs certificate indicating the nature and quantity imported, and further, that the product bears a label satisfying the requirements of German health law. The German courts referred the issue to the Court of Justice, requesting a ruling whether the requirements of German law were in breach of Article 30 and, if so, whether they might be justified under the public health exception in Article 36. The Advocate General examined the residual competence of the Member States in the context of the incomplete state of harmonisation of product licensing requirements. He recalled the Court's ruling in *Schumacher* in this context, and went on to find that fully harmonised Community rules on labelling etc were not yet in operation. Member States therefore retained the right to impose certain requirements, provided, however, that any national rules complied with the two principles of objectivity and proportionality. According to the Advocate General, the German rules satisfied only the first of these tests. Public safety could still be assured, not only by labelling requirements, but by means of various other regulations already in force, including the rules governing both manufacturing and product marketing authorisations. The Court confirmed this interpretation of Articles 30 and 36 (judgement of 16 April 1991).

It should also be noted that in a separate series of cases dealing with restrictions on food additives, the Court has been cautious.[15] In Case 97/83 *Melkunie*,[16] it held that where available scientific findings did not make it possible to lay down precise common standards, it was up to Member States to set their own criteria, subject always to the principle of proportionality. The Court has also allowed Member States to insist on additional testing or to apply different criteria to take into account national variations in diet[17] or climatic conditions.[18] Where the product's particular qualities meet a real need, however, especially a nutritional one, the Member States must authorise marketing. Much depends on the nature of the tests and the standard of safety to be ensured, although it is clear that mere differences in national safety standards cannot be relied upon in themselves to be sufficient justification to exclude an import.[19] Even where Member States are authorised in specific Directives to subject products such as vitamins, for example, to pre-marketing controls, the principle of proportionality must always be respected.

Where there is partial harmonisation of test criteria, the Court is more demanding. For example, in Case 274/84 *Motte*[20] the Court ruled that although an evaluation of the health risks which a particular additive may represent may have regard to habits prevailing in the importing Member State, this evaluation must take into account the result of international scientific research and any non-binding recommendations of the relevant Community scientific committee. In the absence of binding rules and effective supervisory measures at Community level, the national authorities retain full responsibility for the protection of health in their state. This formulation was further elaborated upon in Case 304/84 *Muller*,[21] which concerned the importation from Germany into France of foodstuffs containing unauthorised emulsifiers. The Court ruled that in assessing whether the marketing may present a risk to public health, Member States are bound to take into account the results of international research and the work of the relevant Community committees, in the light of the eating habits prevailing in the importing state. In Case 176/84, the *German beer case*, the Court ruled that where a specific additive is authorised in another Member State, it must be authorised in the case of a product imported from that Member State where, in view of the findings of the relevant international and Community scientific bodies, and in the light of the prevailing habits in the importing state, the additive does not present a risk to public health and meets a real need, especially a technological one.[22] Furthermore, throughout this line of cases the Court has stressed that such authorisations have to be provided under a procedure which is easily accessible to manufacturers and traders.

This case law would seem to support the conclusion that, in the absence of complete harmonisation, Member States are entitled to continue to rely on Article 36 as a justification for national safety licensing regimes. But, in accordance with the principle of proportionality, administrative procedures for imported products lawfully placed on the market elsewhere must be accessible to traders, take account of equivalent levels of protection in the originating state, and be implemented in accordance with the duty to bring about a relaxation in controls on intra-Community trade. Furthermore, in the absence of harmonisation, national authorities must nevertheless assess the scientific data presented to them in the light of non-binding Community guidelines, having regard to local habits and traditions.

A requirement for partial mutual acceptance, but not automatic mutual recognition, can therefore be inferred from this case law, and it would seem that Member States will be entitled to continue to rely upon Article 36 (or the 'rule of reason'), subject to the proportionality test, until Community harmonising measures provide either 'an unconditional set of assurances'[23] or 'a complete and exhaustive set of guarantees'[24] for the general interest. Where the original product has been subject to the proposed decentralised mutual recognition procedure and admitted to the respective markets of the various Member States, it can be argued that this level of harmonisation has been achieved. Hence, parallel imports of products licensed via the decentralised route probably cannot be subject to a separate licensing procedure at national level.

## Patent protection: the new proposals

Even if substantial advances are made to harmonise national licensing procedures, a continuing barrier to parallel importation will be the exercise by the original manufacturers of their industrial property rights. One side-effect of the new centralised and decentralised licensing procedures should be noted. Manufacturers will be able to submit only *one* brand name to the new Community Medicines Agency or for consideration under the decentralised procedure. This will remove the sort of problems which arose in the UK a few years ago, leading to litigation in the *Wellcome*[25] case and to referral to the European Court in the case of *R. v. The Pharmaceutical Society.*[26] At the same time, however, the Commission's latest proposed Regulation on the Supplementary Protection Certificate will undoubtedly complicate parallel trade.

Currently, the duration of patent protection in most European countries is 20 years from the date the patent is filed. Pharmaceutical manufacturers protest, however, that they cannot exploit their patent until they have obtained a marketing authorisation, a process which may take up to seven or eight years. Hence they argue that *effective patent protection* is much shorter than 20 years, which puts them at a disadvantage *vis-à-vis* Japanese or American manufacturers. The Commission had in fact already taken a favourable attitude to these claims. Directive 87/21/EEC introduced, without prejudice to patent protection, a mechanism which prevents a so-called 'second applicant' for a marketing authorisation from presenting an abbreviated application for a period of 10 years from the first authorisation for marketing the product in the Community.

The new system is designed to create a protection certificate *sui generis* in the form of a supplementary protection certificate, which will be granted by the patent office in each Member State at the request of the holder of a national or European 'basic' patent relating to a product authorised to be marketed in the state concerned. The certificate confers the same protection as the basic patent, but protects the product (by which is understood an active substance) covered by the authorisation only until the expiry of the basic patent for all authorised pharmaceutical uses. The proposed Regulation covers only *new* medicinal products. It does not involve granting a certificate for *all* medicinal products authorised to be placed on the market. A new process for manufacturing the product or a new application of the product may also be protected. The protection given by the certificate begins at the date on which patent protection expires and the total duration of the protection must not be greater than 10 years. The Regulation will apply to all products protected by a patent which have not yet received a product safety authorisation. It will also apply to all products authorised after 1 January 1984 and to patents which expire after 1 July 1992.

The new proposal has met with considerable degree of criticism. Unlike the US proposals, which aim at patent restoration, the EC Commission's proposal is in reality a form of patent *extension* which will protect inefficient as well as efficient research-oriented companies. The new certificate will obviously delay the onset of competition from generic products. Furthermore, given that different products will have obtained marketing authorisations at different times in various countries, the effective period of protection offered by the certificate will vary considerably from one country to the next. In Case 341/87 *EMI*

*Electrola v. Patricia Import and Export* the Court ruled that disparities in the duration of protection periods under national law may justify restrictions on intra-Community trade under Article 36 'if the protection period is inseparably linked with the existence of the exclusive rights themselves'.

Finally, the manufacturer may still rely on the extensive copyright and trade mark rights to protect the original product. It is perhaps to be regretted that the Commission has not looked more closely at the question of the 'effective monopoly' via trade mark and copyright rights which a manufacturer enjoys after a patent has lapsed,[27] an area in which substantial divergences remain between national systems. The first Council Directive to approximate the laws relating to trade marks was adopted in late 1988, but does not come into effect until December 1991 (or December 1992 if the Council takes action to that effect).[28] This Directive is limited in its coverage, but represents a major step in that its stated aim is to ensure that the conditions for obtaining and continuing to hold a registered trade mark should be identical in all the Member States. The Directive thus provides a Community definition of a trade mark (Articles 3 and 4) and of the prerogatives attached to the right (Articles 5–9). It incorporates the concept of 'exhaustion of rights', as trade marks remain national rights. Article 7(2) restates the line followed by the Court in *Hoffmann-La Roche* to the effect that the trade mark holder could prevent the importation of goods placed on the market in another Member State, if the goods were subject to repacking of a nature to affect the original state of the product. This restriction is particularly important for parallel imports of products dispensed in their original packs when, for example, new English-language labels and patient package inserts may be required.

## Conclusion

Parallel importation is perhaps a temporary phenomenon, but it is likely to continue for some time, as long as price differences and currency fluctuations provide the economic incentive. At the same time, Member States are making a more concerted effort to 'claw back' some of the profits which pharmacists make from substituting parallel imports for locally manufactured products. This process, which is of course governed by Community law, may remove the existing economic incentive.

The process of importation remains subject to a large number of national controls imposed in the interests of public health, but which are likely to diminish in importance as the Community makes progress towards complete harmonisation. Nevertheless, the continued disparities in national laws on industrial property rights (which are apparently exploited to the full by the original manufacturer) will continue to constitute an important obstacle to parallel trade and to the development of intra-brand competition. The Commission's latest proposal on the supplementary protection certificate will delay the introduction of inter-brand competition. It is to be regretted that the Commission has not addressed this latter issue more fully.

## Notes

1. BEUC/Test-Achats Study on Comparative Pharmaceutical Pricing and Reimbursement Policies, quoted in *Agence Europe*, no. 5033, 10 June 1989.
2. Commission, *Completing the Internal Market*, Com (85) 310, June 1985, Annex, pp 17–18.
3. EEC Council Directive 83/570, O.J. L332/1, Article 15(2).
4. The potential application of Article 100B is considered in detail in my article in the *European Law Review*, 1990, vol. 1.
5. Case 8/74 *Dassonville* [1974] ECR 837; [1974] 2 CMLR 436.
6. [1976] ECR 613; [1976] 2 CMLR 271.
7. See further the Advocate General's Opinion in Case 32/80 *Kortmann* [1981] ECR 1980; also, L. Gormley, *Prohibiting Restrictions on Trade within the EEC*. Amsterdam: Elsevier, 1985, p. 157.
8. Case 120/78 '*Cassis de Dijon*' [1979] ECR 649; [1979] 3 CMLR 337.
9. See, in particular, the Court's recent judgments in Case 369/88 *Delattre*, judgment of 21 March 1991; and Case C60/89, *Monteil and Samanni*, handed down on the same date.
10. Case 247/81 *Commission v. Germany* [1984] ECR 1111.
11. Cases 87–88/85 *Pharmacie Legia v. Minister for Health* [1986] ECR 1707; [1987] 1 CMLR 646.
12. Case 215/87 *Schumacher*, judgment of 27 March 1989, 7 ECR.
13. [1981] ECR 3277; [1982] 2 CMLR 497.
14. See also the earlier Case 27/80 *Fietje* [1980] ECR 3839; [1981] 3 CMLR 722; and the more recent Case 188/84 *Commission v. France* (woodworking machines) [1986] ECR 431.
15. See also its case law on pesticides, where the same underlying principles appear to have been applied: Case 54/85 *Mirepoix* [1986] 1067.
16. [1984] ECR 2367.
17. Case 53/80 *Essen* [1981] ECR 409; [1982] 2 CMLR 20.
18. Case 174/82 *Sandoz* [1983] ECR 2445, at 2463; Case 54/85 *Mirepoix*, loc. cit.
19. Case 178/84 *Commission v. Germany*; and Case 176/84 *Commission v. Greece* [1986] ECR 1213 and 1216.
20. [1985] ECR 995.
21. [1986] ECR 1511.
22. The 'need' aspect may have implications for attempts to implement a so called 'rational drugs list', where drugs are authorised only if there is a proven need for them. Such a test is presently applied in Norway. In accordance with the provisions of Directive 65/66, in assessing the 'need'

aspect it would seem that national authorities might be entitled to take into account only medical and scientific criteria. Questions of cost, for example, the 'need or justification for a more expensive product' cannot be considered within the context of a licensing procedure: Case 301/82 *Clin Midi v. The Belgian State* [1984] ECR 251.

23. Case 72/83 *Campus Oil* [1984] ECR 2727 at 2751; [1984] 3 CMLR 544. In Case 227/82 *Van Bennekom*, the Court observed that 'it should be stressed that Directive 65/65 constitutes only the first stage in the harmonisation of national laws' [1983] ECR 3883, at 3899.
24. Case 28/84 *Commission v. Germany* [1985] ECR 3097, at 3123; [1986] 3 CMLR 579.
25. [1983] 3 CMLR 95.
26. Case 266/87.
27. [1989] 3 CMLR 301.
28. Article 16, O.J. 1989 L40/1.

# 13 | European drug regulatory integration

## Keith Jones

*Chief Executive, Medicines Control Agency, London*

## Introduction

The Medicines Control Agency (MCA) has great interest in assisting the development of international harmonisation in the area of drug regulation. Furthermore, it wishes constructively to assist the birth of the new system for drug control within the European Community (EC).

I would like to approach the subject of European drug regulatory integration along the lines of:

— what we wish to achieve;
— what we have achieved;
— where we are going from here, and the timeframe within which we expect to achieve harmonisation.

Before considering details of the integration achieved so far, it might be useful to examine the goals and objectives in terms of European registration procedures. Our commitment is to the achievement of the single market in pharmaceuticals, and our goals must include the provision of safe and efficacious medicines of high quality, at the earliest opportunity, which offer benefit to patients and thereby to the public health. Additionally, the desire is to encourage trade in pharmaceuticals and to encourage pharmaceutical research and development.

It might also be worth briefly to examine the important reasons for differences which may occur between Member States. These are primarily attributable to variations in assessment procedures, medical practice and terminology, legal status of medicines, prescribing patterns and national laws. All these have been addressed during the process of harmonisation which has been taking place during the past 25 years.

I shall deal only with medicines for human use. A great deal has already been achieved in this regard since the first and most basic pharmaceutical Directive was adopted in 1965 before the UK joined

157

the EC. The process is still not complete as there are further proposals in the pipeline. I will, therefore, outline developments that have taken place so far and look forward to what still needs to be achieved.

The thalidomide tragedy in the 1960s demonstrated a need to control the marketing of medicinal products for human use in the interests of protecting public health. In the UK, this resulted in the Medicines Act of 1968.

## The European pharmaceutical Directives

The first European pharmaceutical Directive (65/65/EEC) was also introduced as part of the regulatory aftermath to the thalidomide disaster. Its objective was to ensure that before medicinal products were placed on the market, they should be proven to be of good quality, safe for patients and efficacious for the therapeutic indications proposed. The Directive intended that this should be done by means which would not hinder the development of the pharmaceutical industry or disrupt trade in medicinal products within the Community. Since 1965, other Directives have been issued to provide detailed interpretation of the requirements of 65/65/EEC and to lay down rules for expert reports, harmonisation procedures, manufacturing and inspection, and to establish procedures for biotechnology and high technology products.

### Directive 75/318/EEC

Directive 75/318/EEC lays down the technical information on analytical, pharmacotoxicological and clinical testing which must be supplied with marketing applications. It also defines the criteria by which competent authorities, such as the MCA, must evaluate applications.

### Directive 75/319/EEC

Directive 75/319/EEC set up the Committee for Proprietary Medicinal Products (CPMP) and introduced the so-called multistate procedure. This was an important new departure, and represented the first step towards real co-operation at Community level whereby Member States were asked to consider divergent licensing decisions taken at national level. It has not worked as well as first thought, despite refinements (I shall come back to this). This Directive also required Member States to review all medicines which had been authorised for marketing prior to the introduction of Community evaluation standards, and to bring such products into line by the middle of 1990. The UK is in the throes of completing this task; it has completed the review of medicines except for a few final details, and has recently wound up the work of the advisory body (the Committee for the Review of Medicines) created for this purpose.

*Directive 87/22/EEC*

Directive 87/22/EEC was the next significant Directive, introducing the so-called concertation procedure for new products derived from biotechnology. It widened the role of the CPMP, and provided for harmonised opinions prior to the issue of any national marketing authorisation. Although CPMP opinions are only opinions, and therefore not binding, in most cases they have led to an agreed summary of product characteristics, with the same indications and conditions of use throughout the EC. With hindsight, this Directive was, therefore, an important step towards centralised decision making (of which more later).

*Extension Directives*

In 1989, four further Directives (the Extension Directives) were adopted, bringing into the scope of Community law additional categories of medicinal products. The general Directive 89/341 amended Directives 65/65, 75/318 and 75/319 and extended their scope. It also dealt with the requirements for patient information leaflets, manufacturers' licences and export licences. The additional categories of medicinal products were vaccines, toxins or sera, and allergens (Directive 89/342/EEC), radiopharmaceuticals (Directive 89/343/EEC), and blood products (Directive 89/381/EEC). This leaves only homoeopathic products outwith EC legislation, and the Commission has now submitted a proposal concerning these.

The Extension Directives require Member States to review all previously licensed vaccines, sera, allergens and radiopharmaceuticals between January and December 1992. It is envisaged that the work will be done in close co-operation between the Member States to ensure that, as far as possible, the quality, clinical indications and contraindications are agreed for products marketed in a number of them.

**Current and future legislation**

This brings us up-to-date with present Community legislation. The CPMP has also formulated various guidelines. In a move towards harmonisation it is understood that no Member State will issue independent guidelines, but will work with other Member States in the preparation of a Community guideline where this is required. These guidelines are approved by the CPMP after formal consultation with industry, and provide clear guidance to applicants. They also prevent any national difference in interpretation of the requirements. Although not mandatory, applicants are advised to comment on and justify any deviations from their recommendations. Guidelines already adopted cover:

1. Data required in support of applications.
2. Technical aspects of the testing of medicinal products.
3. Good manufacturing practice.
4. Good clinical practice.
5. Development of a European drug master file.

Further guidelines have also been drafted, and are currently the subject of formal consultation. Particulars of all application dossier requirements are set out in *Notice to Applicants*, also produced by the CPMP, and which needs frequent revision.

Much progress has therefore been made towards harmonising marketing authorisations across the EC. The UK has played a leading role in this process, and will continue to take an active part as the outstanding proposals to complete the single market in pharmaceuticals are negotiated.

I will briefly outline proposals for current and future developments. First, draft Directives under the heading 'rational use of medicinal products' were issued by the Commission late in 1989 dealing with:

1. Wholesale distribution (to harmonise the status of wholesalers and to define clearly their obligations).
2. The legal status of medicinal products (to harmonise throughout the Community the process by which medicinal products are classified, eg prescription-only).
3. Labelling and packaging leaflets (to ensure consistency throughout the Community of information given to patients on and in the medicine pack).

These proposals are still under negotiation in Brussels, but the Council of Ministers is expected to agree a 'common position' shortly.

In June 1990 the Commission issued a draft Directive on advertising of medicinal products, on the grounds that advertising has an impact on the free movement of medicines in the internal market. This draft Directive proposes rules covering advertising to the general public and to health care professionals. In addition, it relates to activities such as publications, conferences, samples, gifts, and visits by medical representatives. This proposal has been under negotiation since January 1991; the Commission hopes that a common position will be reached before the end of the year.

## Future licensing arrangements

The most significant of the outstanding proposals are those for the future licensing of medicinal products in the EC. As part of their preparatory work, the Commission Services of the Directorate-General III (Internal Market and Industry) engaged in an intensive consultation process involving Member States and the Pharmaceutical Committee, the CPMP and the Committee for Veterinary Medicinal Products (CVMP), for industry the European Federation of Pharmaceutical Industries' Associations (EFPIA) and the European Proprietary Medicine Manufacturers' Association (AESGP), health professionals and consumer groups. In March 1988, the Commission issued a report on the activities of the CPMP and began its first discussion. In April 1989 a second consultation document entitled 'Memorandum on the future system for the authorisation of medicinal products in the European Community' was issued to Member States and other interested parties. This document identified a number of specific Community concerns which included:

1. The possibility of European concertation with innovatory companies during early phases of research and development, and the pooling of scientific expertise for the evaluation of innovatory products between the Member States.
2. A single scientific evaluation valid for the whole Community — a so-called single Euro assessment.
3. Direct access for companies to a Community-scale market for major products, whilst maintaining local/regional authorisations for other companies.
4. A credible system for European marketing authorisations (the 'Euro-MA').
5. The single management of renewals and variations to Euro-MAs.
6. Co-ordination of Community obligations, such as pharmacovigilance, good manufacturing practices (GMPs), good laboratory practices (GLPs), good clinical practices (GCPs), etc.
7. An updating and harmonisation of testing requirements.

Finally, proposals were submitted to the Council in November 1990. The package consists of one Regulation and three Directives. Briefly, the main features include the establishment of a new European Agency for the Evaluation of Medicinal Products. This would be a new administrative entity, the responsibilities of which would include: co-ordinating assessment work, supporting the CPMP, co-ordinating pharmacovigilance, maintaining GMP, GLP and GCP, and supporting a pharmaceutical data bank. The proposals also include the creation of a new centralised Community procedure for the evaluation of certain biotechnology products and, optionally, other products of significant EC-wide interest. They also include a decentralised procedure, based on the principle of mutual recognition, applicable also to extension of existing authorisations, and a proposal that national regulatory authorities should continue to evaluate applications for products intended for their sole market.

The proposed implementation date is January 1993 for the centralised procedure, while implementation of decentralised aspects will be phased between January 1993 and January 1996. Substantive negotiations have not yet begun, and I have the impression that a lot of work needs to be done in a very short space of time. It is always possible, of course, that the Commission's timetable may slip.

The UK has been closely involved with the development of these proposals and supports the principle of some form of central decision-making process. Indeed, it is widely known that the UK was invited to submit a document outlining the structure and possible function of a central agency. Increasingly, since the development of these proposals, the concertation procedure has begun to work and to deliver Community decisions and licences.

An analysis of the CPMP concertation procedure shows that over the last six months the CPMP has reached a unanimous position on the seven major products which it has considered. For each product, it has been able to agree the summary of product characteristics to be used across the European Community. The procedure for the approval of variations is also working satisfactorily. This represents a major improvement upon the earlier experience of the concertation procedure. The experience also compares favourably with the operation of the multistate procedure. The present performance of the concertation procedure might lead some to suggest that the need for a central agency could be questioned if such good results can be delivered by the present co-operation between Member States. It should also be remembered that in the concertation procedure the applicant is able to choose the rapporteur, an issue on which many in industry have strong views.

However, the proposals need to be fleshed out before we can be satisfied with the outcome. In particular, they are vague about:

— the relationship between committees, experts, the central agency and the agency's executive director;

— the political, legal and scientific liability for regulatory decisions;
— how the centralisation of pharmacovigilance arrangements will work.

The MCA intends to play a constructive role in negotiations, and will press hard to obtain agreement with other Member States on basic criteria. Our overriding concern is to ensure that any proposals for future systems are achieved through a carefully phased implementation that matches responsibilities with capacity and performance, and minimises dislocation to the industry. We shall also seek to include adequate regulatory, scientific and medical expertise among the CPMP membership and revisions to the proposals which clarify the powers and duties of the EC agency and its director in respect of the CPMP. We will wish to ensure that future systems include both adequate opportunity for dialogue between applicant and assessor and between applicant and the final scientific decision-making body. We have reservations regarding the feasibility of a central adverse drug reactions reporting system, and are concerned at the possibility of duplication between national and central function. This should be reduced or avoided, at least until electronic data exchange is available.

On a global basis, the success achieved by the EC in harmonising data requirements and other arrangements has given added impetus to consideration of other markets, in particular Japan and the USA. The International Conference on Harmonisation (ICH) will take place later in 1991 and will offer an opportunity for the EC to discuss common ground with representatives from these two countries with regard to marketing arrangements.

## Conclusion

To summarise what has been achieved so far, I think it is fair to say that we have come a long way since the first EC Directive in 1965. The EC has enhanced its standing in international markets and has shown other countries how successful co-operation at a multinational level can be. Of course, there is still much to do before there is truly a single market in medicines, but we are learning from past mistakes and gradually building on our experience to increase the greater chance of success in the evaluation of our future programme.

# 14 | Summary

## Joseph M. Thomson
*Regius Professor of Law, University of Glasgow*

---

In attempting briefly to summarise this meeting, I shall mention only four major topics. First, the regulation of the conduct of research. Professor Kennedy raised the extremely interesting theoretical issues of consent and also introduced the problems posed by the European Community (EC) Guidelines, which were expanded upon by Mr Hodges. In relation to legal liability when something goes wrong, we are to some extent taking a sledge-hammer to crack a nut, given the success there seems to have been in the very few cases where volunteers have suffered injury or illness as a result of research. Much more important, of course, particularly in the light of what we have heard in relation to the EC, is the value of EC Guidelines in terms of the interchangeability and the acceptability of the data discovered as a result of the research.

The second topic, of particular interest to a lawyer, is the problems facing potential plaintiffs and pursuers who have suffered injury as a result of drugs or other medical interventions. I have a lot of sympathy with Mr Milne's contention that since the ideal solution of no-fault liability will not be achieved in the foreseeable future, the thrust of reform should be to try to improve as best we can the existing system of civil liability. No-fault solutions may well be theoretically interesting, but in practice they are difficult to achieve. It is well-known that the New Zealand no-fault system has suffered immense financing difficulties—and, indeed, some people take the view that it is now defunct.

It is very important—in fact, vital—to remember the importance of legal procedure. It is by reforming our legal procedure that we can attempt to aid the working of the existing system by reducing the currently appalling delays etc in litigation.

Mr Dodds-Smith raised the interesting and new (at least for Scots and English lawyers) idea of multiparty litigation, particularly in relation to the situation in which perhaps thousands of potential plaintiffs have suffered as a result of something going wrong with drugs or other medical devices. I shall await with great interest the result of the new procedures which are being introduced in England to deal with this multiclaimant type of litigation. My rather sceptical view is that it will cause immense difficulties. Here perhaps there may be value in looking at the approach taken in the USA where such actions have been going on for many years. The judge takes a much more interventionist role in the litigation process, and can seek to set up a trust fund and simply distribute the monies to all the plaintiffs on a 'take it or leave it' basis.

Thirdly, may I reiterate the remarks of Professor Burrows to the effect that today we are all being European lawyers. It is easy to forget, for example, that the Consumer Protection Act 1987 was intended to implement an EC Directive—and there is to be an EC Regulation in relation to research trials. I think it is important to have had the opportunity to concentrate on areas of substantive EC law rather than on UK law which has been passed to implement EC Directives.

In relation to the European presentations, my first thought is how difficult European Community law is. For example, the problem of parallel imports is fascinating: it is a technical area of law, yet it raises immensely difficult questions not only of law but of economics, and it also illustrates the importance of the jurisprudence of the European Court. There has been a tendency at this meeting, quite rightly, to concentrate on European legislation, but the most important part played by the European Court of Justice in many areas of European law generally must not be forgotten, in particular in this area of parallel imports.

My second thought is how complicated, as opposed to intellectually difficult, is a lot of the EC legislation—and what a lot of it there is. It is almost impossible for any private lawyer, however specialised, to keep abreast of the sheer mass of legislation. This is slightly worrying—and brings us back to Professor Kennedy's point that the more detailed the Regulation the more difficult it is to keep up with it. At the same time, we may be so concerned with the trees of detail that we lose sight of the wood of principle that we are trying to follow. If the founders of the European Economic Community in the 1950s were alive today, they might well be surprised by all the detailed legislation necessary to achieve their aims for the original Community.

My fourth and final point is what might be called a professional law for pharmaceutical physicians. The question was raised in discussion about criminal, as opposed to civil, sanctions being used to regulate the pharmaceutical profession. I have doubts about the effectiveness of bringing the criminal law into this area. To take a (not very good) analogy, the criminalisation of certain acts which constitute insider dealing has not, I think, been a success. It will be interesting to see whether there will be a large number of prosecutions in relation to pharmaceutical physicians. I hope not.

Perhaps not surprisingly, legal liability rather than legal responsibility was discussed. The medical profession generally is clearly concerned about and acutely aware of the minimum legal standards within which they are obliged to operate and to which they must adhere. I hope and trust that these minimum standards are seen to complement and not conflict with professional standards.